A Good Dad's Guide to Divorce

A Good Dad's Guide to Divorce

One father's quest to stay connected to his children.

John McElhenney

MCELHENNEY
AUSTIN

A Good Dad's Guide to Divorce Copyright © 2019 by John McElhenney. All Rights Reserved.

Contents

Preface   ix

Introduction   1

Section 1: The Beginning – To Become Parents

The Transformation of Love and Parenting in Marriage and Divorce   7
John McElhenney

The Joy of Young Parents   10
John McElhenney

Section 2: Struggles and Distress in a Young Marriage

The Love Hurricane: Becoming Parents   13
John McElhenney

Are You Receiving Me? When Not Listening Turns Towards Divorce   19
John McElhenney

Section 3: Compounding Issues and Fracture

At the End of Sex and the End of My Marriage   27
John McElhenney

Letting Go of Broken Things: A Marriage Comes Apart John McElhenney	33
The Odyssey of the Single Father: Kids Change Everything John McElhenney	37
Blameless Divorce: I Had a Dream Where You Apologized John McElhenney	42
The Training and Education of a Reluctant Divorcé John McElhenney	46

Section 4: Divorce, Anger, and Loss

What "Responsible Separation" Means John McElhenney	51
Rising Again From a Depressed Silence John McElhenney	56
Divorcing With Kids: The Golden Rule - It's About Time, Not Money John McElhenney	60
Inviting the Dinosaur Into Your Divorce John McElhenney	64

Section 5: Freefall and Depression

Minimizing the Collateral Damage of Depression and Divorce John McElhenney	70
A Good Man in a Storm, Even After Divorce John McElhenney	74

Losing Everything Again, And Finding Happiness Anyway John McElhenney	79
Divorce Lessons: It's the Quiet Time, the Alone Time, the Empty Spaces John McElhenney	83

Section 6: Loss Is Part of the Journey

Dear Daughter, We'll Catch Up on Thursday John McElhenney	89
Transformational Divorce John McElhenney	92
Bad Daddy and the Delicious Breakfast Dilemma (A Single-Parent Fable) John McElhenney	97
Displacement: A Single-Parenting Love Story John McElhenney	101

Section 7: The Core Promise of the Single Parent

Continuing Forgiveness As a Single Parent John McElhenney	107
Prayer for All Single Parents, and Especially My Co-Parent: Humans of Divorce John McElhenney	113
Going for Gratitude With Your Co-Parent, No Matter What John McElhenney	117
Cultivating Low Reactivity as a Co-Parent John McElhenney	120

7 Wins for the Hyper-Focused Single Parent John McElhenney	122

Section 8: The Recovery Path Back to Happiness

How Long Will it Hurt? Divorce Recovery, the Road Back to Happiness John McElhenney	126
The Good Side of Divorce - Making Things Go Easier John McElhenney	131
Thriving After Divorce: 6 Life Hacks Along the Recovery Process John McElhenney	133
Holding Your Dream Together as Your Marriage Comes Apart John McElhenney	138
Single Dad Writes to his 16-year-old Daughter About the Divorce John McElhenney	143
Every Single Day at a Time John McElhenney	153
Epilogue: Hope for the Good Dad	158
The Single Parent Manifesto: Love All Parents John McElhenney	159
Resources	163

Preface

One father's journey to staying connected and engaged with his children before, during, and after divorce.

Nothing can prepare you for the grief surrounding divorce. And with children, the divorce is never final; your relationship to the other parent goes on as long as your kids are alive. You never get over your divorce, but you can get through it. And in this book, I am going to show you how to thrive after divorce. My hope is that this honest retelling of my experience helps guide the way for your future adventure into becoming a single parent. I am a good dad, I worked at becoming one, and I continue to work in my children's lives to remain a constant and positive force in their lives. This is my journey.

Introduction

Every action I have taken since my then-wife asked for a divorce has been to protect and serve my children. Often at my own expense, I've gone along with the requests of my co-parent. Having kids changed everything for me: being a good dad would define the rest of my life.

+++

The most devastating moment in my life was when I was asked to leave my family. My then-wife wanted a divorce. She'd been planning for months, apparently, but had failed to bring her issues into couple's therapy. I was asked to leave the family. She would've liked me to have left that day, telling the kids I had to go away on a business trip. How many dads have been disappeared over a "business trip?" It's an easy explanation. It happens all the time. Daddies have to go away for business. And in a divorce, it is most common for the daddy to have to go away as well. She was exhausted, she was at the end of her rope, and she was certain my presence was what was making her miserable. I'm pretty sure there were other causes, and I was hopeful that therapy would help… That's not how it went down.

It was April of 2010, and I was asked to get out of the house and give my then-wife and the kids some time to rest and recover. Even our therapist thought it was a reasonable request. I did not. In my parents' divorce, my dad was asked to leave (for his alcoholic behavior and rage), and we struggled on as a little family of two after that. But it was awful. It was never the same. I never recovered from the loss of my father.

Then I became a father. I was determined to be the "best

father" and never give up, never quit trying, and never abandon my family like my father did. When the axe did fall on my neck, I was unprepared for the emotional impact of the loss. I met with a trusted therapist days after my then-wife requested a divorce. I sobbed. I was distraught. But I was not sobbing for me or the marriage. I was sobbing for what my kids were about to lose. I knew what losing my father had done to my life, to my sense of myself as a man. I knew about the challenges my son was going to face when I was effectively removed from 70% of his life. And my daughter, I knew less about her inner needs, but I felt her pain even more deeply, as she asked on the day we told them, "What animals are you going to take with you?"

I think she wanted to make sure I got an animal to go with me, to keep me company.

In the end, it took me over a year to recover from the depression that ensued and find a place I could afford to live. I had a new job, a new outlook on life and my potential in it. And, finally, my kids could come and live with me on my 1st, 3rd, and magical 5th weekends. It wasn't enough. I was starving for time with my kids. I could tell they too were suffering from the stress of the divorce. I could tell they were missing my jovial attitude towards life. My loving and positive influence no longer inhabited their daily lives. I was only available on alternating weekends. Monday through Thursday every week they were with their mom.

In the fallout from the divorce, I could feel my son grow hard against me. It was as if I had decided to leave them. I suppose that's the story we told them. "This is what's best for all of us. Your mother and I have decided to get a divorce." Except that wasn't true at all. I had fought against the divorce. I had asked her to reconsider her decision several times over the summer. I had pleaded with her not to break up our family.

I know my kids missed me. I know my general happiness and loving morning routines getting them up, fed, and off to school were missed from their weekday lives. We were never the same.

I never gave up, however. And even as my ex fought against my survival and eventual resurrection, I stayed as close as the Standard Possession Order (SPO) would allow me. We all tried. Even my ex-wife, in her defensive and angry heart, gave my fathering a priority pass, when it fit with her agenda. She did her best to keep the kids available to me during the off parent times. She would allow them to call me or accept my phone calls every night. She tried to remain cheerful as we passed in the kid handoff logistics. But she was not cheerful. She was not happy. She took the divorce, the divorce she asked for, bitterly. And my kids saw her bitterness. Some of that bitterness remains in their perspective about me, Dad, and the divorce.

How could they know, even now, that I did not choose, but fought against the divorce? They don't. How could they know their mom has routinely acted against me in random and angry outbursts? They don't. How could they know that she methodically destroyed my financial solvency through her actions? They don't. That's also part of the burden of being the dad and being asked to leave. We have to put on a brave face and say it was our idea, our decision, too. And we have to act like everything is going well, even when we are crushed inside. The kids don't need to worry about their dad. So their dad stays strong, gives positive reports about life after the divorce, and stays supportive of their mom, even when she's behaving badly.

As I was asked to leave the house, and I told the kids it was also my idea of what's best for all of us, I was aware that it was a lie. The divorce was the single biggest disruptive event in my life. My entire trajectory for my hopes and dreams was altered by one woman's decision. All of us were changed forever by her act of self-preservation. I'm sure she was fighting for her life as she asked for the divorce. But that's her side of the story, a side I'll never fully understand.

The courts in the state of Texas see the dad as the ancillary parent and the mom as the core parent. Dads make the money, moms hold down the emotional support. That's not how it worked in our family. That's not how we parented. That's not what I asked for, as my one demand in the divorce: "We should share a 50/50 schedule with the kids."

I know my kids roamed the empty divorce-house seeking my happy soul. I know my ex suffered from depression as well and that the divorce was hard on her emotionally. I know that their side of the story after I left (what it was like in the house after I was asked to leave) might never be told. But kids' emotional connection to their dad is essential for all of us to understand.

The dad is also important in a family. A dad's energy and vitality are essential to the balanced growth of kids. When I was removed from the family system (70% of the time), my positive lifestyle and emotional intelligence vanished from a good portion of their lives. This is why I grieved when my wife asked for a divorce. This is what cut so deeply when my father left the house for the last time. Even as an alcoholic, he was my dad, my masculine, rough-house playmate. And when he was gone, an emptiness, a longing entered my life that has never quite been fulfilled.

We need our dads to show up for us, as well as our moms. And when the dad is removed from a family, with the SPO, the balance is shifted dramatically in favor of the mom as the emotional center of everyone's lives. My dad was unable to provide any emotional closeness as he continued to actively pursue his alcohol addiction. As I left my kids' lives for 70% of the time, telling them it was also my idea, I left them without the positive and hopeful center I bring to life. I left them with an emotionally challenged mom.

I respect and honor the hard work my ex-wife has done being a mother to our kids. I do not think my kids got the best deal by having me removed from 70% of their lives. Today, I would fight for 50/50 parenting with all my heart and soul. I would fight to remain in my kids' lives at the maximum level allowed by law. What I got was 30% instead of 50%. I believe that 20% difference would've had a beneficial effect on both my kids and me.

In this book I hope to provide guidance for dads and moms about how to maintain a healthy process throughout the divorce experience. Of course, the experience never ends. Once you are divorced, you are on your own. I struggled, I failed, and I continued to recover and reinvigorate my relationship with my kids. That's the best I can do going forward. May this book help you find the postive thread in your divorce and the future health of your kids.

Section 1: The Beginning – To Become Parents

Setting your dreams for the future family you are to become. Negotiations. Trials and tests. And a miracle: you are pregnant.

The Transformation of Love and Parenting in Marriage and Divorce

John McElhenney

Parenting, the act of having kids, changes everything.

There are two types of parents.

1. The parents who are prepared to have their lives transformed and welcome the new kid-centric lifestyle.
2. The parents who attempt to maintain their pre-parent lifestyle, often at some expense to the kids.

My ex-wife and I gladly gave our nights, weekends, and all available energy to the wondrous transformation. We saw some of our friends choose the other path. It was an odd thing to see them molding their child to fit into their training schedules and work routines.

As you continue to grow with your kids, you continue to change with them. As they get older, they begin engaging with you in more ways, andat this point the two parenting paths reflect in the relationships that form.

We agreed about our parenting style. The love hurricanes entered our lives, and everything was torn up and rebuilt around the parenting life. Of course, it transforms parts of your relationship to your spouse as well. As a dad, I was often competing for time with my wife. Not competing really, but negotiating. Trying to find ways to give her more time, more energy, more space so she would want to be intimate again. That's what I wanted but often not what she wanted. And that too was okay. I remember a moment, before kids, when my wife and I were talking about going ahead and trying. "I'm ready to not be the center of my own life," I said. "I'm a bit tired of my own shit."

Then, making the decision to have a second child, even after the massive re-organization of our lives, was a step even further down the path of transformation. As the new child was born, I was thrust more directly into childcare, both of my son and of the newborn. We all became intimate.

Again, the transformation was good. Nothing that had worked before would still work with two kids. There were timing issues. One would be sleeping while the other was cranky and inconsolable. One of us parents would take the waking child while the other tried to get a nap in. We worked together and often marveled when things worked. "One for each of us," we joked. But there was some truth to the equation.

One-to-one parenting may be the best ratio. You get to give 100% attention to your child. What they play, you play; what they want, you provide; what they are afraid of, you to explain, and so on. And our little unit grew in leaps and bounds, and things changed again and again in response to their needs and our desires to keep them well-fed, well-schooled, and well-parented.

Until the unbelievable happened. In all the work to keep the kids at the center, we lost some of the relationship between me and my wife. We lost some connections that were not easily restored. As parenting duties continued to mount, we were less and less able to put in the effort to rejoin. Things between us headed down a very functional but less-than-compassionate road. We still parented with all our hearts, but we didn't couple much.

I don't think it was an easy decision for either of us. But in the end, when we decided/realized that divorce was probably the best option, we worked together, as we had to create these wonderful kids, to create a positive divorce. And we failed many times over. But we kept coming back to what was most important, the kids. So it goes, with so many busy parents; the kids came first, and the relationship suffered. There simply was not enough energy and love to go around, and at some point, the idea of divorce was introduced.

I believe that our child-centered lifestyle and choices allowed us to let go of the marriage in favor of the kids' welfare. Regardless of who blinked first in the marriage, in the end, it was a mutual decision. And we have always worked (well, mostly) together to keep our marital and then co-parenting issues out of our kids' lives.

We've all suffered and we've all gained something from this transition. But neither my ex-wife nor I have put anything before our kids' welfare. I can thank her every day for the great job she is doing as a single parent. Somedays I wish it hadn't happened, but I always wish her well. It's not easy. It's a challenge when issues come up. But if we both really resolve to do what's best for our kids, we come around to co-parenting, and loving co-parenting at that.

I still love my ex-wife. It's different, of course; I don't want to be remarried to her. But she is doing a great job at a difficult task. It was almost impossible for me to imagine happiness again when the marriage began coming apart. But here we are, both reasonably happy, with super happy and intelligent kids. And for that, I give thanks to her and my resilient kids.

The Joy of Young Parents
John McElhenney

I saw this couple today with their young child and I was inspired again. What kinds of things were going through our minds when our children were between the ages of 1 and 5? Amazing times! Amazing growth in them and in both parents, rediscovering their own lives. Everything changes when you have kids, that's a given, but the sheer joy of becoming a mom or dad cannot be understood by those who have decided against having children. (It's just a choice.)

How do we lose the magic? When do our kids turn into pain-in-the-ass teenagers? When does their great upbringing and nice upper-middle-class lifestyle become a liability rather than a gift? I've been in that place recently, trying to weigh my love of my kids and and temper it with the patience required to keep sane while they are forgetting things at their mom's house, forgetting to tell me about a dropoff that needs to happen. While you ALWAYS love your kids, parenting has definite levels and plateaus.

I think my kids and I are just entering into a new phase. Something beyond mere teenager angst and into something that contains the fascination and joy at simply being a parent. I noticed in this young couple today, the way they had already begun to ignore their girl. And then how they returned to 100% focus on their little jewel. Somehow I had drifted away from the real appreciation of my kids.

It's subtle. Chores, work, exhaustion... It's good we feel so much overwelming love at the same time we are facing overwhelming changes in our lives. And somewhere along the way, we think "I got this," and we handle our kids just like we see everyone else handling their kids. Yes, they are a priority, but life goes on, and priorities shift.

In the last three years my kids have drifted in and out of my life. I always get my "every other weekend," but I don't always appreciate it as I should. I get bogged down in "Jesus, all she wants is a ride somewhere."

Today, I could appreciate the love and joy and in-and-out focus of these young parents. I could see myself as a new dad. I could feel the change that overcame me in the first hours of my son's arrival.

And I woke up a little bit. I have a 15-year-old boy and a 13-year-old girl, and sooner than I think they will be away at college. What can I do in the years ahead?

1. Let them know they are a priority in my life.
2. Give them the confidence to move forward with their dreams.
3. Provide all the advantages in life I can while helping steer them in the direction of gratefulness.
4. Hold strong boundaries and high expectations.

I can be present, I can be honest, and I can be vulnerable with them. Today I saw the joy and blessing of a little girl with her mom and dad. I saw myself 10 and 15 years ago. And I woke up.

Section 2: Struggles and Distress in a Young Marriage

How parenting changes both partners. You did not marry this person your spouse has become. Adjustments and readjustments. Finding boundaries and reestablishing the love between you and your spouse.

The Love Hurricane: Becoming Parents

John McElhenney

Everything you might read or hear about becoming a parent pales in comparison to the storm of emotion and the life-altering moment your child gasps for their first breath, making their presence and frustrations known. The love hurricane will rip through every aspect of your life. You can either lean into the transformation or you can push against it.

There seem to be two distinct approaches to becoming parents. Either you allow the experience and responsibility to completely transform your life and priorities into the phrase "kids first." Or you push back against the transformation and embody a more "and now we have kids" tone. In terms of parenting philosophy, the first "transformative" approach would be aligned with attachment parenting. The second approach tends to compartmentalized the parenting experience so that it doesn't alter the pre-parenting lifestyle too much.

From the moment we started trying to have kids, our approach was "all in." Even a part of our courtship and fairly rapid marriage was a result of both of our commitments to becoming parents, together. We knew it was one of our highest purposes in life. And when we met and fell in love, the parent path was part of the passion and plan that heightened our relationship.

We joined a Bradley Method class and began to join in the dreaming and planning for the actual birth experience. I remember the Thursday evenings driving out to the class with my pregnant wife, talking and holding hands on the 30-minute trip. We were beginning the visioning for the coming of our child. I also began a dialogue with our unborn child as I patted and encouraged the little soul arriving in my pregnant wife's belly. It was a sublimely spiritual experience, this prepping for the love hurricane. Rather than battening down the hatches, we were cracking open our previous lives and making way for something amazing to happen. We had no idea.

This is no *What to Expect When You Are Expecting* process. The books help very little. The advice from friends and your parents is well-meaning, but more about the storyteller than what your experience is going to be. If you are tuned into the experience, and tuning into each other as a couple, you know this already. And the overwhelming feelings of joy and fear and togetherness mix into a new bond between you and this third being. Already, we were beginning to change, to get closer, to become dependent on this new interconnectedness. We were never going to be the same. We let the feelings heighten the process. The three of us grew some sort of spiritual connection beyond any church or prayer experience we'd ever been through. We were prepping the way for the hurricane.

Then it happens, the rush of arrival beginnning with my wife's water breaking in the middle of a Tuesday afternoon in October. We had a magical moment between us as we cried and laughed and called our doctor and our doula. We had set our birthing plan ahead of time, and we knew our doctor was committed to letting us take the process as naturally as possible. He gave us the day and most of the night together alone with our experience and asked us to come into the hospital around 4:00 a.m. on Wednesday if the contractions didn't start.

We went for a last walk around our neighborhood as parents-to-be. We held each other in bed and rested, too excited to sleep but tired enough to cuddle together as we waited.

Our son arrived around 10:00 a.m. Wednesday morning.

Everything changed.

I never let my son out of my sight. I traveled with him to the warming room with my hand on his back, to his heel prick, where he wailed for the first time, and back to his mom, where he learned what breasts were all about. That first night I curled up at the foot of the bed in the hospital and kept a hand on both my wife and my child. "Here we are," I kept saying, in prayer. "Thank you, God." It was a mystical experience, this arrival, that transcended any religious experience or knowledge in my life. It was one huge prayer of thanks, for 36 hours.

At the moment you arrive back home, the hurricane actually takes control of your life and all the things you used to do. The house becomes a laboratory. The bedroom becomes a classroom, a study in breasts, poop, kisses, sleep, and crying.

We found a healthy routine fairly early on and, against the advice of our parents, attached a little sleeping bed to the side of our bed, in a co-sleeping approach to parenting. I'm sure both of our parents would've preferred some sort of crib and detachment process. My wife and I had studied the theories and fallen in love with the idea of attachment parenting and co-sleeping. It was controversial at the time but in line with our love and our ideas of what we wanted for our kids.

Maybe this is where the distinction between the two kinds of parenting starts. In attachment parenting and co-sleeping, you make a commitment to remain close to the child, giving them the controls about when and how they migrate out of the family bed. Sure, it's less conducive to returning to the previous routine, but it was easy for the two of us to invite the love into all corners of our lives. We couldn't imagine anything more loving than being a family.

Alone time and private space could be found later or in different ways. We lept into the "big bed," as our room became known, and have never looked back. Our pre-parenting lives and bedroom no longer existed. Our bedroom became a place for family, sleeping, cuddling, wrestling, tickling, and joy. The love hurricane had blown through and given us the happiest moments we could ever imagine.

In these early weeks, we befriended several other couples with new babies. Our little community of new parents became our new tribe. We had one other couple who were easily identified as attachment parents and a handful of others who were more traditional. It was an interesting process getting to be with them and watch the differences in parenting styles that we were each making up. Parenting styles must come partially from our family of origin and partially from what we read and learn about "how to parent."

One couple, in particular, was obviously "we're going to fit this child into our lifestyle" parents. Occasionally when we were together the differences between the way we related to our kids was striking. It seemed perhaps that our son was running amok over our lives, while our friends seemed to have a more organized and disciplined routine.

One of the early examples was the fenced/gated play area they had set up for their child. It was convenient to keep all the balls and toys and messiness in a small corner of the dining room. However, something about it felt too controlled. There was an aspect of the messiness of our connected relationship with our son that seemed quite different from this more controlled or regulated approach. And we learned pretty early on that you don't talk "attachment" to parents who are taking the other road. Co-sleeping might appear almost abusive to people who don't lean that direction. With one couple we celebrated our interconnected chaos and closeness; with most of the other couples, we observed a more restrained expression of love and caring.

I'm not here to argue for attachment parenting, but I do believe that an overly controlled experience of becoming a parent short-circuits the transformational process a bit. I can see the benefits to keeping your pre-parenting life on course a bit more than we did, perhaps, but I think the 100% emotionally connected approach is what ultimately gave both our children their warm and loving personalities. They are joiners. Of course, they are still young, so we've yet to see much of their lives as teenagers, but they appear to be extremely resilient and emotionally centered.

And when their attached parents became divorced, I believe it was this closeness, this "two big beds now instead of one" approach that carried us all through the process with little or no visible scarring. We all suffered. We've all spent time alone that we might have preferred to be different. But the attachments we established early on, as touchy-feely, messy, inclusive parents, are also the glue that keeps us connected now that we've been a fractured family for over four years.

When your children arrive, you either allow your life to be torn apart and reassembled by the love hurricane, or you fight to maintain aspects of your pre-parent lives as you push back against the transformation. It seems to me that our "closeness" approach allowed us to survive the divorce in a loving and connected way. Perhaps it is even some form of "attachment divorce" that is what keeps me on the loving and positive path as a divorced dad.

Allow the hurricane to arrive and blow away the old aspects of your lives. Reset your expectations and parenting lives around the love and support of your children. Then, even if things don't work out with the marriage, the closeness and love that you've established with your kids becomes the strength and bond that guide your relationship even after divorce. That experience of closeness also becomes the approach your children will use as they begin to establish relationships for the rest of their lives. That's what I understand and appreciate even now about my ex-wife. I can celebrate our approach to becoming parents and how we welcomed the messiness and transformation of staying closely connected.

John McElhenney

What causes couples to stop listening to each other?

In the beginning of your relationship (remember the courtship phase), nothing was sweeter than the sound of your new sweetheart's voice. It didn't matter if you were both talking about work, or a movie, or what you were looking for in a long-term relationship. The sound of their voice and the way they looked at you was enough to send you to the moon, to make you believe, to give your heart the final push to let yourself fall in love.

And falling was easy. They said the right things, they wanted to be with you as much as they could, they reassured you of your attractiveness to them and their fidelity to your burgeoning relationship. All was bliss and planning and discovery.

How and why does your lover's, partner's, coparent's voice become less intriguing? And when did they stop listening to you all together? Was there some event? Was it a gradual falling apart?

In my marriage we listened and laughed our way through the courting and falling in love phases rather quickly. Right place, right time, I guess. And then somewhere along the way, our words no longer conveyed the caring and love they once did. Sure, we had a lot of conversations about chores and bills and delegation of tasks and errands. But along the way I was still constantly reaching back towards the love expression we once shared. I was writing love poems and love songs. I was doing the best I could in the marriage, but I was still reaching to bridge the widening gap between us with words of love. Sure, doing the dishes or vacuuming was more concrete than a love poem, but it was the whole experience we were grooving on.

I have tried many times to unravel the past and see just where the inflection happened and we veered off into ignoring and isolating rather than enjoying and celebrating. A very specific moment and series of events began the fracture that eventually became our divorce.

I had been working at a big corporate job for two years, and suddenly the 2009 economic reset downsized the entire company, taking most of the creative people and over half of my group out. It was a hard blow, but they gave me six months pay with insurance to soften the landing.

When they told us about the offer in November, I immediately began planning for my next career move. One of the things I started right then was a blog about the social media marketing that I'd been doing for this international tech company. I had always been a writer, and the blog became my megaphone for my career ideas, my business marketing ideas, and my real-world experience lessons in trying to use social media to generate revenue.

The blog took off. I had a few early hit posts that began building a readership. And I worked Twitter like a fiend, imagining it as the next real force in marketing. But something happened at the same time to the communication and trust in my marriage. I remember the lunch we shared when our divergent perspectives and ambitions clashed in the bright clear February day.

"Well," I said, "It seems like I have six months to figure out what's next."

"No," she said, "It's only about $30,000, and that really doesn't get us very far."

I was stunned. "Wait. What?" I was happy about the

opportunity to retool and find a job with a bit more work/life balance. I was recovered from the job loss and on to my trademark optimism about the future. She was building her spreadsheets and being very pragmatic about the dollars and expenses and what she felt was a very risky period for us.

The reason, I came to understand later, was she really wanted me to just get another big corp job and be back on the path we had been on for two years. I was 20 pounds heavier and completely burned out and was looking forward to reframing our lives in a different way. I could not just go back to the corp job grindstone. I had to find a better job, a better way to earn a living. And we had to work together to make a sufficient income to live the life we had established.

Over the next few weeks, we worked on this disagreement in therapy. We built our own spreadsheets in Excel and exchanged ideas about what we envisioned for our future. But we couldn't quite reconcile the two opposite ideas. Her: just get another great job. Me: I want to find a more healthy way to earn a living.

She also started taking aim at my blog, saying I was being mean or saying things that might come back to haunt me when I was looking for the next job. I didn't agree at all. I was building a new potential for employment. I was blogging with the intention of selling my expertise as a consultant. I was also picking up momentum with the posts and began building an audience. I picked up a few consulting gigs at this time, even as I was looking for work in the traditional way. The next job eluded me. I had interviews. I was getting the response on my résumé that I wanted, but something wasn't putting me in the HIRED column.

A few months after our initial meltdown, it began to happen. She had always been good at expressing her anger and frustration, but she was really beginning to let me have it. Complaints were an acceptable form of behavior modification, but her complaints became rages. She occasionally blurted out, "F*** you" in a moment of frustration. And it was as if her anger was spilling over beyond her ability to contain it. Why she wasn't getting at this with her individual therapist I don't know, but she was certainly trying to work it out with me.

At one point she told me point-blank that she wasn't in love with me anymore. She was giving me a warning, "You'd better listen to me. You'd better pay attention to what I'm saying. I am not happy."

I tried to be zen about it and cooperate and respond while continuing to go about my merry way, in terms of job hunting, consulting, and blogging. But my positive attitude seemed to signal to her that I was not taking her threats and warnings seriously. I was, and I wasn't. We were in couples therapy. We were in a committed marriage. And we were having some problems. No problem. We'd work it out.

Somewhere deep inside me, I was solid in my belief in the marriage. This was just a difficult period that we would get through, as we had done so many times before. I remember saying a couple times, "I don't really like you right now, and I know you don't like me, but I love you and am committed to this marriage. We'll get through this tough time." That is what I believed. That was also the basis of my confidence and positive attitude in the midst of all this obvious angst on her part. I KNEW my marriage was solid, the details would unfold, and we could repair the relationship as we went along.

It was from this confidence in my relationship that I was still writing love songs and poems to my beautiful wife. Sure, my beautiful wife was frustrated with me 24/7 and wasn't interested sex at all, but we'd get through this. I was sure of it. And I was calm in the face of her escalations and demands. I think that might have made her even angrier.

I wasn't all that calm inside. I was hurt by her words. I was sad that she was not responding or even smiling at my songs and poems. Sure, words are not enough, but I was doing everything I could around the house to be the best husband and father that I could be. I had been stepping up my partner-in-chores role for over a year. I also felt like I was putting in 100% percent to the marriage. And part of that contribution was not responding in kind to her outbursts. I was hurting and feeling abandoned and isolated, but the inner commitment to my marriage and parenting with her was unsullied.

It was from that confidence that I began to express my own dissatisfaction with the relationship. It had been several months since the money/severance conversation, and I had landed a new big corp job. All the requests from her had finally been fulfilled. We had enough money, I had the big job with benefits and retirement contributions. I was still over-performing as a responsible parent and homeowner.

It wasn't enough for her. Nothing shifted. Even when there was money in the bank, and money coming in, and a maid to help with laundry and general cleaning, she was still madder than hell at me. As I began to realize that all the things she used to be mad at me no longer applied, I was expecting some of *her* joy and intimacy to return. With all the conditions of satisfaction met, she was still as frustrated as ever.

Guess what? It wasn't me that was making her mad.

So I began to express my own frustration and disappointments. I wanted to revisit our sex life in therapy and understand where she had gone. I wanted her to get her own anger issues under control so we could rebuild our friendship and trust.

Under these stresses and disconnections, I lost the big corp job after just four months. Sure, it was a serious blow, and I had a case against them for discrimination, but I knew we would recover.

On top of everything she was going through personally and the festering anger at me, the job loss without reasonable explanation was too much for her. She snapped. All the threats and complaints she had been lofting at me suddenly made 100% sense to her. I was an unreliable breadwinner. I was killing my opportunities through my edgy blog. And I was not changing into the person she wanted me to be, so… She was done.

Within a few weeks, we were negotiating a divorce rather than strategizing a rebirth of our love. I was unprepared for the revelation that she had been to an attorney to consider her options for divorce. I was blindsided. Not because I was happy. No, I had been expressing my own dissatisfaction for the first time in our marriage. I was blindsided because I had no concept that our MARRIAGE was in trouble. I was still 100% committed to our marriage. And it was from that belief and joint agreement that I felt confident to stand up and state what I wanted in the relationship.

When the other partner decides, however, there is very little the committed partner can do. The fracture has happened. The other person has declared they are considering divorce. Then that option is forever on the table and could be used as leverage. I'm considering divorce if you don't… If you won't change, I'm going to divorce you.

I was not what was making her mad. I was also not capable of making her happy or of making her want to stay in the marriage. Once the "talked to a lawyer to consider my options" card had been laid on the table, all bets were off. I had no more confidence that the solidity of our relationship was capable of withstanding some readjustments.

It seems crass now to say it, but in the end, I believe she just wanted me to go back and get the corporate job. It allowed her to freelance and spend time at the kids' school as a volunteer. And when I declared that in the long run that was not going to be my path, that I would get the job but was planning a move to something else, she was faced with the reality that I wanted her to contribute fully to our financial needs so that we could *both* live a more balanced life. That was enough to break up our family and seek greener pastures.

We had a ton of emotional and practical issues between us, but in the end, I was demanding a change and she was claiming that I hadn't changed enough. I actually think she wanted me to continue pulling in the big bucks regardless of the health impact on me. It was definitely an easier lifestyle for her.

Section 3: Compounding Issues and Fracture

Money woes can take a toll on any relationship. Roles and responsibilities in the family can become challenged as the kids grow older. And the financial changes in the economy or the primary breadwinner's job status can wreak havoc on a fragile marriage.

At the End of Sex and the End of My Marriage

John McElhenney

Let me set a few ground rules, as I like to be 100% positive. Sex and sexual dysfunction are a partner thing. It wasn't her fault. It was our fault. And sex, in my opinion, and the opinion of a lot of relationship experts (though I'm not one), is very important to a marriage.

For me, sex bonds me, it makes me feel connected, close, warm, loving, proud. Sex is like the glow on the relationship. It's both a reward and a gift. Sex can be about giving and focus on the other partner. Or sex can be about receiving and doing your best to shut down the mental rap sheet of expectations and performance. Or sex can be a dance between two people, like a tango, or waltz, or punk rock slam dance.

It's all good. It's all about sex, baby, it's all about you. and. me. Let's talk about sex.

Early in my courtship, sex was magical. The moment my emerging girlfriend candidate told me, "I went to the doctor today." She was grinning ear to ear. She knew what she was about to give me. "I got a prescription for birth control."

Oh my. I might have been hooked into marrying her from that very second that the warm glow rushed into my body. "We still have to wait about a month for my cycle, but it's a start."

I was thrilled. We were thrilled. She was saying YES PLEASE, let's do it.

And things early on were just as good as that first rush.

Playful. Exploratory. Loving. Fun. And somewhat frequent. All was right with the world, with my sex life (as a man), and all was heading in an upward direction. The "Life is Good" shirt applies here and was worn frequently, as was my just-done-it smile.

Another magical milestone was crossed on our honeymoon. We were getting married in an ancient church in a tiny French town, and the night after a major lunar eclipse, we decided to start having sex unprotected and without birth control. She had been off the pill for two months or so...

We knew what we wanted. But the moment we decided and had newly unprotected sex again, with the intention of bringing a child into the world, well, the sex took on a whole new level of awesome. It was as if a spiritual purpose had taken the joy and expression of our love to another level.

Onward we sailed into the newly married bliss of frequent and unprotected procreational sex. It sounds like a mouthful. It was heaven.

Our son was born less than a year later. And with a few months of off-limits self-reliance, we were back in the bedroom making up fun stuff to do with her newly arrived breasts. More joy. More interruptions and laughter and coupling. And more unprotected, sure-let's-have-another-kid sex. More play, more connection, more fantastic sex.

I'm going to skip the drama around our daughter's medical issues and the fact that 9-11 ripped out all the joy from the world. But the stress of the world took its toll on our joyful sex. We still attempted it, we were told not to go for a third child, and we were okay with a perfect pair, boy and girl. And the closeness was still there when we found the windows for alone time, when neither of us was too exhausted to do it.

And of course that's a thing. Marriage, kids, financial obligations, and chores really wear down both parents. It's typical for one parent to take on the worry and stress more than the other parent. (Often men are picked on for being less responsible, or not growing up, but I can assure you that's not what was going on between us.) I was 100% present and accounted for. I did the working-for-a-living dance. I mowed the lawn, picked up toys and rooms, did some cooking, and loaded and unloaded the dishwasher, and we were both still tired.

Now, more often than not (a lot more often), any indication of sexual readiness on my part was met with a sigh or an eye-roll, depending on her level of exhaustion.

I learned new ways to ask. The playful, "Hey, how about I give YOU a blow job tonight?" The suggestive, "I'd love to give you a back rub as soon as I get the dishes done." And the supportive, "Is there anything I can do to make things less stressful for you, at this moment?"

But somewhere in her hard wiring, the stress had shut down her sensual response. We went to counseling, but mostly that was about some crisis or another that we needed to work through. We never really addressed the sex thing; I was trying to be a stand-up and selfless husband in support of his wife. I have no idea what she was doing. But we were doing it together and not "doing it" very much.

And then one last magical thing happened. With the full insurance of my job, I got a vasectomy. Hallelujah. It was like a new ON switch for our sex life, perhaps not how you might think.

The mechanics of a vasectomy have one similarity to birth control for women. Once you have the procedure (or get on the pill), you have several months to wait before enjoying your newfound freedom. In the case of a vasectomy, it's not time, but ejaculations that count down towards the miracle of unprotected non-procreational sex.

And it was as if my then-wife's libido had suddenly been jump-started back into gear. We didn't have a schedule or chart or anything, but the mental count in our heads, once I was healed enough to be back in action, was like a shining green number above my head. Forty ejaculations. Then you had to see the doctor again, give a specimen, and have it examined for viable swimmers.

It was as if the mythical Spanish Fly was being introduced to my wife's tea and coffee every day. We treated it like a sport. In the shower. BOOM. In the morning before getting out of bed. DING. And any time the kids had dropped off before us. BINGO.

It couldn't have been more than 45 days and we were making our appointment with Dr. Let's-Get-It-On again. We leaped into the world of parents with small children who can now do it as often as they like and not worry about having any more kids. It was a maturing process for sure. I was pretty young to be getting a vasectomy. WE WERE INTO SEX, AND WE WERE GOING TO HAVE A LOT OF IT. That's what I imagined the vasectomy was saying about us and our future love life.

But…

Well, I'm sure you can guess the story. Things fizzled after a few months with no goal. We joked about setting another objective, a milestone to "shoot for." But it never happened. And, in fact, without going to far into the intimate details, it started to go way South rather than back towards loving, touching, squeezing.

We checked everyone's meds. I read a few books, tried a few things, asked in more creative ways. Nothing.

Now, the real story is probably much deeper than the sex. And I have tried to ask, both in real time while the collapse was happening, and later in therapy when things were really bleak.

We didn't talk about sex anymore, even in therapy, because the "issues" had become seemingly insurmountable.

But I still wonder if I had protested more, if I had demanded that my wife work to refind her sexual center again, rather than being self-consoling, I might have penetrated the fog that had taken her intimacy out of the relationship.

Again, please understand, I AM taking responsibility for my part in the dance that began to come apart. And again, I'm really not saying that sex was the primary ingredient that caused us to get divorced.

What I am saying is at the end of sex our marriage was also closing down. The sex might have been a conduit for us to rekindle the loving feelings for one another. The love-making was certainly a part of my DNA and the primary way I felt loved. Well, not just sex, but physical touch. And we did have some of that. But when a back rub is the only way you get to be touched by your beautiful wife, even when you are jumping through every hoop introduced, things can begin to get a bit off track, distant, disconnected.

I believe some fracture happened during the course of our financial and medical struggles that broke some trust inside my wife. And while I can't put my finger on it, and I am merely projecting my hindsight reflection, which is most definitely NOT 20/20, I know she closed down her sexuality. She might not have done it consciously. But as she began to contemplate or imagine life beyond our marriage, it was necessary for her to stop giving herself to me in a sexual way.

The first time when we were making love during this period, when I noticed things were off, I caught her looking out the window, seemingly bored. "Are you okay?" I asked.

She snapped back to awareness of the moment. But the moment was despairing. Clearly, a disconnect was happening during our lovemaking. And we were done. And maybe, in some internal way, for her, at that moment we were really done. Done in a much bigger way.

Letting Go of Broken Things: A Marriage Comes Apart

John McElhenney

After a while, divorce became no longer the most important feature/event in my life. Yes, it's still the most transformative event in my life. But I don't think about my ex-wife and our fallout that much, anymore. I think that's a healthy thing. We're parents first. Other than that, I don't really have much to gain from a relationship with her.

I wanted it to be different.

I had dreams, when we were first arranging the divorce, that we would be friends. Friendly even. For reasons I don't comprehend, that has not been the way my ex-wife wanted things. Something in her past got triggered, and she got angry at me. Eight years later, she's still mad at me. And not in an abstract or indirect way. My ex-wife, bless her heart, is still lashing out at me in random acts of madness. I don't know what she's mad about this week. The good news is, I don't have to know. And, in fact, her anger no longer concerns me.

I am sad that my ex-wife has so much unresolved anger. I'm sure it's not a great environment for my kids. But there's not much I can do about either of those things, except be a good father. I can't really be a good ex-husband to her, because any contact with her is fraught with barbs and jabs that come out of left field. There is no sense to her anger. And yes, I'll admit, it still gets to me, but it's really no longer my concern, nor my business, why my ex-wife walks through life with a chip on her shoulder.

Unfortunately, I'm afraid my kids have a less positive perspective on life as well. The word *cynical* was important to my ex-wife. She did not think things were going to work out between us. Even as we were going to couples therapy, she used the word "cynical" to describe her perspective one day as we were driving to our session. My word was "hopeful." Wow, we were living in different relationships. And I believe the relationship we have with another person is a deep reflection of the relationship we have with ourselves.

Somewhere along the road to becoming an adult, my ex-wife was hurt badly. Her anger today is more likely related to her past hurts than it is to me or my actions. I mean, we don't talk or interact at all, so I'm fairly certain that she is not being triggered by my actions. But she is upset. I'm sorry about that. But I don't think it's my doing, and I know it's not my responsibility.

When you are married to someone who is angry a lot, you tend to adjust your behavior accordingly.

- I learned to not ask for what I wanted.
- I learned that her problems were more important.
- I learned that a crisis meant we both had to focus 100% of our energy on that issue.
- I learned that love/sex/closeness could be conditional in a relationship (not a healthy one, however).
- I learned that even by being the "best boy I could be," I was not going to make her happy.

I don't like to focus on my ex-wife much anymore.

My kids are the big feature, the top priority in my life. How can I support my kids? What actions can I take that would support them? Can I do things to get closer to them?

When we focus on our ex-partner and the co-parent of our children, we may begin to have those codependent feelings again. We may imagine that we have responsibilities that we no longer have. And we must learn to let them go completely.

There is nothing I can gain from my ex-wife.

- I don't need her approval, her attaboy, or praise.
- I don't owe her anything but respect and consideration (even if I'm not getting the same from her).
- Her anger doesn't involve me (I didn't cause it, can't control it, can't cure it).
- If I can focus solely on the happiness of my children, I can let go of any attachments I have/had to my ex-wife.

This letting go is a healthy part of the process of divorce. Yes, we're all hurt and resentful when a marriage comes apart. But as we separate and get clear about our own issues, and our own responsibilities, we learn, we come to understand that we are not responsible for another person's happiness. And thus, we are also not responsible for their anger.

I owe my ex-wife a debt of gratitude. But I no longer have to stand in and weather her stormy moods. As I learned during some of my divorce recovery work, you can treat your ex as you would a convenience store clerk. You go in, you ask for what you need, you complete the transaction, and you leave.

At this moment, exactly eight years to the month when my then-wife let me know she had been to see a lawyer about her options, I am able to fully embrace her as a co-parent and reject her anger as an ex-wife. I'm done with that label, I'm done with her influence and power over me in my reaction to her mini-rages, I'm done with her as an angry partner. I am no longer a partner with my ex-wife. Unfortunately, that means I am also no longer a communicative/loving partner with my co-parent, either. That's not the way I saw this whole co-parenting thing going down, but it is not all up to me.

Co-parenting is a cooperative relationship. When one of the partners decides to be uncooperative, it changes the dynamics. However, as a positive parent, you can be the bigger partner. Choosing the positive is about every aspect of your life, and your kids are the most important relationship you can manage. You cannot manage the relationship with the ex-partner. In fact, you must let go of your dreams of being in a loving co-parenting relationship. It's okay if that's not going to happen. I'm a bit sad about the loss of this partnership. But, it's not in my best interest to continue trying to navigate her choppy waters. I'll sail around my kids and navigate within their spheres.

The Odyssey of the Single Father: Kids Change Everything

John McElhenney

A radical transformation happens in your relationship the minute you both decide to have children. The act of welcoming the chaos of life into your lives is courageous and life-altering. When the first love hurricane arrives, nothing will ever be the same. Your priorities change. Your goals and ambitions are altered and curved back towards your kids and your idea of "family." It was the most ecstatic moment of my life. I leaned into the spiritual rebirth and reconnection with God, my wife, and my new son.

If we could stay in that frame of mind, as parents, divorce would never be an option. But, as it goes, life changes, kids grow and multiply, and before you know it the stress levels are getting out of control and someone is unhappy about the marriage. The dream is still in place. The family is still the focus of your life. But something more individually critical is changing. One parent is losing optimism, becoming resentful of some part of the duties that have become a burden rather than a delight.

But make no mistake. Parenting is a delight. It is your own individual journey, your own individual life experience, that frames up your experience as a parent. Both of us put 100% of our lives into raising our two young children. From couples birthing coach classes to pre-natal screenings, I was alongside my partner the entire time. And we chose attachment parenting as our strategy for keeping things on track, creative, and full of loving-kindness. And as we all grew and learned, we stayed close and connected as a young family.

We also split duties along traditional lines, and my wife stayed home for a good portion of the time after our first child was born, while I continued the traditional working-dad role. With our second child, we experienced some major medical challenges, which began to fray the hopeful feelings of our relationship just a tad. It was as if the stress floor in our lives was being gradually increased each week. On Monday mornings, we'd visit the neo-natal surgeon's office to determine our daughter's medical prognosis.

During this period I experienced a major crisis of confidence. I simply lost the ability to reassure myself that everything was going to work out. The inner voice that had been with me my entire life, saying "You're going to be okay," was no longer present. I white-knuckled the next few months until our daughter was born, with therapy and drugs doing their best to reconstitute my confidence. But a full-blown adult-onset depression had kicked in and affected both my life and my wife's life at the same time. I cannot imagine having a partner being so crushed right beside me, while I was depending on them for so much. I give thanks still to my then-wife, for standing beside me, even as she was about to give birth to a second child.

And then we were in another blissful period of hovering and rallying around a newborn girl. Even our son, two at the time, began to get with the program in a new way. We had some months of "new family bliss." I continued to work out of the home, while mom stayed with the kids for the first nine months. We got a maid and a nanny to help with the overwhelm of two children and a busy household. And we soldiered on in our relatively stable and happy home. The damage, however, had already been done. The trust and confidence in our marriage had been shaken by both the hardships of my daughter's medical odyssey and my own emotional breakdown.

We continued to struggle with parenting and the financial changes bringing two kids into the world has on a couple. And my work, in social media, was as volatile then as it is now. Companies would hire entire departments of people to hand the "new media" and then six months later shutter the program. It was a hard time, post-9/11, and everyone was still a bit shaky about everything.

There were a lot of hard times. A lot of hard discussions. And, in the meantime, we had a growing and more demanding pair of children. Something in the relationship between me and my wife broke down. We worked on things in couple's therapy, but it was like trying to push a river back upstream. Some fracture had happened during the previous struggles that weakened her belief in our ability to recover and thrive as a family.

My wife decided to consult an attorney about her options. I didn't learn about this until I confronted her in couple's therapy about something she said.

"Have you been to see an attorney about divorce?" I said, frightened and angry.

"Yes, but it was just a consultation."

I was devastated. Why had she not brought that idea into couple's therapy? What were we doing in therapy at all?

Over the following week, she requested that I simply move out of our family home, tell the kids I was traveling on business, and begin the process of divorce. I refused on several counts.

First count: the kids were two months away from completing the school year. (My son was in fifth grade, my daughter was in third.) I refused to abandon my kids or my home before the end of the school year. We could all recover over the summer. The elementary school counselor was the only voice of reason my then-wife could hear. We cohabited until early June.

Second count: I was still hopeful that my then-wife would see the error of her decision as we worked together through April and May. But my resolve was not 100% pure. I was angry, scared, and still deeply committed to saving our marriage. My then-wife was not. She had already shopped the divorce brochure and was making plans for her next life.

Third count: Divorce is also a business decision. In addition to working out the parenting plan, the details of the financial split would take a while to sort through. Would we need to sell the house? How would we pay for two households when we were struggling to keep one afloat?

In the end, I lost all of the arguments about staying in the marriage, about divorcing with 50/50 custody, about keeping our family together. When I left the house in mid-June, I was forced to move in with my sister while I regrouped and found a new, higher-paying job. It takes two partners to keep a marriage together. When the mother of my children lost faith in my ability to maintain gainful employment, she started looking for alternate routes to support her family.

It's odd, but one of our main breaking points was about how to share the burden of our household bills. As I was coming off two years at a high-paying ultra high-stress job, I wanted to renegotiate our earning balance. She did not want to negotiate. She wanted me to get another big job, regardless of the physical or emotional cost to me, while she continued to work 10 – 20 hours a week. Of course, when she divorced me, even with a hefty child support payment, she had to return to full-time work and probably worked harder and longer than she had ever done while we were married. I guess she got what she wanted, but I think a compromise and rebalancing with me might have been a better choice.

It's all water-under-the-bridge at this point. We've been divorced for over eight years. Our son has just turned 18 and is heading to college next year. We're not really co-parenting, but our kids are doing just fine. And as they grow older, they are seeking a renewed relationship with me. Even as I lost 70% of my time with my kids, I never stopped pursuing them and engaging in their lives. I will never stop being their dad.

Blameless Divorce: I Had a Dream Where You Apologized

John McElhenney

I don't want my ex-wife back, but I'd give almost anything to have my time with my kids back. All those nights and weekends where I've had zero access to them other than a phone call. ("Hey, honey, how was your day?" "Good." "Um... Anything cool happen at school?" "No.") I wouldn't consider remarrying her, and I'm sure she has even less interest in that than me, but I'd consider almost anything...

Okay, but I'm daydreaming here. And I saw for a moment, in the dream, my ex-wife coming up to me with a beautiful smile on her face. "I'm really sorry about the divorce," she said. "Yeah, me too." And then she (no she didn't) said, "And I miss you. Would you want to come home?" In the dream, I was intoxicated with joy. I was willing to do almost anything to make it happen. If she'd said, "But there's one condition, you have to scrub the toilets every night until I'm happy with them" I might have considered... But again, these are just fantasies.

I would not remarry or rejoin my ex-wife. I would love more access to my kids. And I would've stayed in a troubled marriage until I was fatter and deader than I was when we split up. I would've stuffed my sadness and disconnected feelings in the name of staying married, for the kids. Yikes! That's not good.

But something in the dream was about forgiveness. Something in the dream was a redemption. That all this pain and suffering that we've all been through was forgiven. I was forgiven. She was forgiven. And I was coming home.

I've blamed my ex-wife for the divorce in the past. When I was in a divorce recovery class, I classified myself as the dumpee and her as the dumper. And for that, I've grown familiar with my tendency to hold her up as the reason we got divorced. That's not accurate at all. It never is. Even when there is a clear dumper and dumpee, a lot more factors go into the loss of love in a marriage. And I'm sure we were no exception.

In fact, I had begun to get pretty vocal about the things that I was unhappy about in the marriage, towards the end of our last year together. I was learning to talk about what I didn't like, as opposed to just keeping quiet in some sort of sadistic Buddhist practice of suffering in the contemplation of my own suffering. I was beginning to give voice to my dissatisfaction. I was learning, for the first time, to get angry. (Anger was something we didn't do in my family of origin. Dad had more than enough anger for all of us combined.)

And my anger and voicing of my own frustrations were not helping things get closer between us. However, I saw a tipping point in my mind, if I could just get to the heart of the fight about our marriage. If we could just dig in and let it out. If our counselor could give us the tools to express, honestly, what we were feeling.

And what if that IS what happened? (I'm having an ah-ha moment as I'm writing.) What if the clarity of our communication was what lead us to actually getting a divorce, rather than staying together in some painful compromise? I hadn't really thought that idea through when I began writing this.

So, I got clearer about what things were hurting me in the divorce. And my then-wife was doing the same. We learned that a complaint was a fine form of communication. We learned that listening and truly trying to hear what the person is saying, rather than thinking of our defense, was the best way to get clarity between us.

When we parted, we agreed to disagree in the ultimate relationship in our lives. Our divorce was based on clear communication of what we thought we needed and what we thought the other person was incapable of giving us.

We met for one last time with our therapist. We needed closure with him and between us. It was decided that we were going to divorce. We wanted to say one last time, with his support and love, what we thought the fundamental issue was that was causing us to seek release. He was not trying to fix us. He was helping us communicate better, and that's how we ended.

I went first: This is a moment in our relationship where have an opportunity to strip back down to the basics. What we want in our lives and our relationship together. I feel like we've been given a warning flare and this is a new beginning. I'm committed to doing whatever it takes to rebuild with a new foundation.

She said: We are two very different people. Things you keep doing are triggering me and I don't feel like anything is getting better. I do not see a future where you are different. And I think I'm done.

When I thought back on that exchange over the years, I've had this feeling that she did me wrong. I see now that she didn't. She spoke her truth. And she had the courage to speak honestly about her desire for a different future.

While I could hold on to this event as her decision to leave the marriage, that's not what it was. We didn't agree on next steps. We didn't see the future in the same optimistic light. I wanted to rebuild. But I was also saying very clearly that things had to change. A dramatic change was taking place, and I wanted to capitalize on this moment and make the leap to the next chapter of our relationship as married partners.

She saw the world through her eyes and didn't want to go on trying to be different or trying to work it out. (In the final two years we spent a lot of time and money in therapy, trying to "work it out.") And it wasn't going to work out, in her mind. Or she wasn't willing to change in the ways I was asking her to change. Either she couldn't or she didn't want to; both are acceptable truths.

We spoke our final piece. We blessed our therapist for working with us and giving us such a safe place to explore our individual realities and how we were trying to find the "fit" between us.

It worked for a long time. I experienced the bliss of love and parenthood with a best friend. That is a truth. And as we grew into our parenting roles, we had different ideas about how that should look. And I fess up, I was unhappy. I was asking for a massive change. In the end, we disagreed on what we wanted as a couple. As parents, we have never disagreed. Today, we're still pretty tight on issues that involve our kids. And I'm happy to release her from any blame I might have been carrying.

We discovered our truths. We learned to communicate them. And we agreed to come apart as a couple but stay close as parents. And that's our life together, without blame.

The Training and Education of a Reluctant Divorcé

John McElhenney

It does not matter if you are the parent who says, "I want a divorce," or the parent who is surprised by the fractious disclosure, your life and the lives of your children will be forever changed. You can't walk that one back.

For me there was no mystery that we were in trouble, the admission came during couple's therapy, but the form and bluntness of the admission were even more devastating. Something she was saying, in response to a question from the therapist, gave me a hint that all was not well. I struck with some sort of defensive instinct. I asked, "Have you already been to see a lawyer?"

That second. When she blushed and nodded. That second began my training to become a divorced dad.

In many ways, I went under the bus with a quiet gasp. I agreed after several sessions more that working together required both of us wanting to be married. One of us didn't.

I cried and wailed, but mostly to my individual therapist. And mostly I was crying about my parents' divorce. I did not ever want to inflict that kind of pain on my kids. And at the outset of our divorce planning, I was determined not to repeat the bitter struggle that defined my third through eighth grade experience of life. Yes, my parents divorced over a long and extended battle. But it wasn't so much about custody. It was about money.

We didn't have a lot of money to argue about. We had debt,

which would come into play later. And we had two kids, a house, and two cars. What we had from the start, and what we continue to put at the front of any of our discussions, is the "best interest of the children." Now, this phrase may come back to haunt you, but there are ways to get over your own pain and continue to be an awesome divorced parent.

Early on we agreed to do our divorce cooperatively. We would focus primarily on the kids and the parenting plan. We'd get a divorce accountant to help us "run the numbers." We agreed to not fight with lawyers. We got through all of those agreements pretty quickly, once I agreed that divorce was the only course of action.

I sometimes try to play the higher/lower game where I blame my ex for the divorce. "It was her idea." But the reality is, I was just as angry and frustrated by our relationship as she was. It was my parents' divorce and the devastating aftermath that kept me terrified of divorce.

Newsflash from the present me to the just-divorcing me, "It's actually going to get better after you divorce. It might take a while. You're going to have to do some work on yourself. But the divorce is the best thing for your situation."

It's no mystery that an unhappy marriage and angry parents breed some pretty unhappy kids. Had my parents stayed married, my life would've looked a lot different. And while it's easy for me to see how their divorce distanced me from my father's alcoholic demise, I could not understand or cope with the loss when I was eight years old.

Things are very different now. Most of my kids' friends have divorced and remarried parents. It's not a stigma for them. We the parents have to get out of the way and let the separation not be a horrible, awful, most destructive thing. Let me say that again for emphasis.

The separation of divorce is not horrible. The divorce may actually be better for all parties involved. It is our reaction and past history with divorce that become the issue. I had a hard time with the divorce. I hated the idea. I fought to keep things together. And in the end I fell into a depression over the loss of my 100% parenting role. All these antics and struggles I needed to go through, I suppose, to finally break down enough to let go.

In the end, divorce is about letting go. But we're letting go of the things that don't work. We let go of the pain that comes from being in bed with someone you love and feeling more like surfing Facebook than making love. We let go of the fantasy that we had when we started the marriage and parenting journey, where we claimed, "We will be different. We will win. We will never divorce."

The biggest transition in my life happened when I lost my marriage. The amazing thing is, out of the other side of this wreckage that I became, I also re-emerged as a writer. The plays and novels I had been trying to write suddenly spilled out in blog posts about divorce and parenting.

What my divorce gave me was the freedom to become who I wanted to be all along. The roles and constraints of my marriage had strapped me into a course of action that was killing me. At my high-paying corporate job, I was gaining weight, developing high blood pressure, and feeling pretty crappy about life. Sure, I came home to the picket fence and the smiling kids, but the wife was not so happy, and dinner was rarely in the oven.

The parenting dream and the American dream and the artist's dream are often set up in opposition. If I can't make a living as a writer or musician, I've got to find ways to make a living and hope that I can keep my creative passion alive in the fragments of time I have left. And parenting was the biggest responsibility

I had, and have. There is nothing more important than my kids... Wait a minute. Let's back that one up a minute.

More important than your kids is YOU. In order to be a good parent, you have to survive. Depression and soul-crushing workloads are not acceptable. And more than survive, you have to show them how to thrive, even under the circumstances that seem dire and depressing. Becoming a stronger person, showing them how I could roll with the punches and get back up as a man and a father is one of the most important lessons I can transfer to them.

Thriving as an artist, even if I don't make a penny from it, is also part of my gift and my message to my kids. You need to know what you want. From there you can rebuild from any setback and regroup, reset, restart.

The divorce was a hard reset for me.

The gift that I was given by my then-wife's admission was the gift of my creative soul. If I had aligned myself towards corporate work and being the good dad with the nice house in the nice neighborhood, I might have really suffered a death. My own creative death, and ultimately the death of many unhealthy white professionals who struggle along with little joy or passion.

I had the joy and passion in spades. I had a misaligned marriage that generated two wonderful kids. Today I have reset myself towards a creatively fulfilling life. I hope that my children learn from my example. Even in the darkest of times we may find the answer we were looking for all along.

My divorce was also my rebirth as a writer and musician.

Section 4: Divorce, Anger, and Loss

I listened to the anger long enough, until she told me her name was grief. When one parent feels betrayed by the divorce, the rage and fire can become frightening. There are no winners in divorce, only negotiations. The imbalance of the divorce process favors mothers in most states, and dads either have to fight for 50/50 custody or be somewhat marginalized by the standard divorce system and the SPO.

Once the divorce brochure has been presented, it is very hard to remain fully committed to a marriage. "Options" become plans and strategies. Anger begins to replace compassion. And as things get more stressed and tense, the greener grass of single parenting may appeal to one of the partners. Once the idea of divorce is raised, the lid cannot be put back on the box of the healthy marriage.

What "Responsible Separation" Means
John McElhenney

Laura A. Munson has written an amazing book about a crisis of heart she and her husband suffered. Well, actually her husband suffered some sort of mid-life crisis, and she was along for the ride. When he said he didn't love her, she didn't buy it. When he suggested divorce, she refused.

She was determined to stand by her husband and her family come hell or high water. And the flood was all around rushing through her house, her bedroom, her life, but she stayed with it. It's an amazing story, and it made me a bit sad when I first read about it in the *New York Times*.

> This isn't the divorce story you think it is. Neither is it a begging-him-to-stay story. It's a story about hearing your husband say "I don't love you anymore" and deciding not to believe him. And what can happen as a result. – Laura A. Munson

What? Amazing. How did I not deserve this same resolve? Even when I was fighting to stay in my marriage the entire time. How did I not have a fighting wife?

Her husband kept falling down his own mid-life rabbit hole of despair, and she kept holding strong to her house, her family, her marriage.

> "I don't love you anymore. I'm not sure I ever did."
> His words came at me like a speeding fist, like a sucker punch, yet somehow in that moment I was able to duck. And once I recovered and composed myself, I managed to say, "I don't buy it." Because I didn't. -Laura A. Munson

And this was only in the short article about the transformation that occurred when she took on her husband's depression with her own fury and calm resolve to never give up on him.

The article is a bit more inspiring than the actual book, but I'll let you go through the entire story on your own. (book: This Is not the Story You Think it Is ... a Season of Unlikely Happiness)

She keeps coming back to the idea of the responsible separation. Over and over again, her husband just wants out, wants something else, wants an apartment in the city. And she gives him some conditions if he wants his responsible separation.

And actually, in my marriage, my ex-wife stood by me with great resolve and strength as I went through my own version of a mid-life crisis and major depression. It's hard to admit to REAL DEPRESSION, but that's what it was. I needed counseling and medication to get up off the floor of the confusing and sad ideas that were clouding my head, much like Mrs. Munson's husband.

We came through the trauma as a family, but the lover in my wife had exited the stage. She was here for the family and no longer hid the anger she felt towards me. It's okay. She had a right to be angry. For a while.

We weathered huge storms, and we came through it. But something, some wounding happened in the process that weakened our marriage. Some element of trust became threatened, and for her, it broke. For me, I was so grateful to have survived both the depression/crisis and the potential divorce that I was hopeful and energetic at the rebuilding of our life and love together.

When anger becomes constant and unyielding, it becomes toxic. Probably more toxic to the angry person than those around them, but it makes everyday life a lot more difficult and dramatic. And the shift was gradual, almost unnoticeable until the flares would shoot out sideways with a casually thrown curse. It was painful and different. We both reacted the first time she shouted at me. Ouch.

And the anger didn't subside. I woke up each morning with a positive approach to things, difficult and easy. She didn't. She was unhappy.

Some of our difficulties in life are participatory. And often our partners are the triggers for our anger. BUT when the anger lasts longer than a few hours, or cannot be discharged, the deeper hurt and anger are with someone else. The core anger is related to our family of origin. And we cannot resolve it with our partners. That work is done outside of our relationships. But it must be done. Or we bring this unresolved BS into all of our relationships.

I can't pass judgment or claim to know what she talked about in therapy, but something was not getting processed. In some form of the story, I was the cause of her hurt and anger. It's not an uncommon story. I know, but here the roles in the Munson story were reversed.

Even after my wife had consulted a lawyer and had told me she wanted a divorce, I was unsure that this was the right course for us and our family. I fought her. I fought our couple's therapist who suggested maybe I should just leave the house and let things cool down.

What?

The concept of separation was proposed, but I was not able to see the value of leaving my house. I was not willing to leave my kids and family two months before the end of the school year (kids ages seven and nine). No way.

The school counselor was actually the one who convinced my

wife to wait, if indeed we were going to divorce, until summer break.

And that's what we did. I stayed in the house, as a roommate. I still got everyone ready for school each morning and made breakfast. And during the day, I worked from my home office trying to figure out how to (a) make more money and (b) convince my wife that divorce was not the answer. I failed on both of those objectives, but I succeeded in keeping my kid's lives relatively stable for the remainder of the school year. It sucked. And ultimately I did not do a very good job at proving myself to be a great partner. I was a great father. But that wasn't the issue.

Somewhere along the hard path, the issue had become trust. When one partner begins to lose trust, the recovery is difficult. And if the distrusting partner is not willing to do the work, the process is doomed. We sat in the last few sessions with our counselor and recounted our two different positions.

ME: We've had a crisis. We're in a great position to rebuild around the core issues that were not working.

HER: I had shown yet again how I could not be trusted. And it was more of the same. I was obviously never going to change.

And in fact, I too was waiting for her to change. And that's never a winning proposition. I knew this already. But I was willing to sublimate my desire for a "touch-centered" love in the name of keeping the family together.

I wanted her to be something different. She wanted me to be something different. We didn't agree to a separation, we got a divorce. BUT, we tried, and continue to try, to make it a responsible separation. We do our best every day as co-parents. That's as good as it gets, once the decision has been made to separate.

+++

Munson, L. A. (2009, July 31). Those aren't fighting words, dear. *The New York Times.*

Munson, L. A. (2010). *This is not the story you think it is ... A season of unlikely happiness.* New York, NY: Penguin.

Rising Again From a Depressed Silence
John McElhenney

She arrived in my life in January of this year.

In February of this year, my life fell apart, due to my own emotional tides, and I slipped into a depression. I did not see it coming. I was on top of the world, and boom, I was freaking the hell out. And then the most amazing thing happened. She stayed close and connected.

See, she had read my blog. She was aware of my emotional fragility and what I had written about the pain of my divorce. She entered into a relationship with me knowing these things about me. Then, even when the proverbial shit hit the fan, she leaned in rather than away from me. She recalibrated. We talked about and examined what we were doing together. I talked about my depression and how it usually affected me. And again, she decided to stick around.

Now the weird thing about depression is when you are going through it, your worldview gets rather myopic. You are so self-focused on what has gone, is going, and will go wrong in your life, that you miss the fact that there are a lot of people around you who are being affected by your emotional flatline. As I was questioning my life focus and my reason for being alive, I had this other person, this new person, who was also experiencing my depression with me. She might have been a bit afraid or sad that the shining prince had fallen ill. She might have run away or given reasons for "things not working out."

She didn't, she stayed.

When she asked what she could do for me, I said plainly, "Just be here. Stay close. Touch me."

She did.

In my marriage, I went through spills and thrills. And while my then-wife did an amazing job at staying married to me and remaining a committed and resourceful mother, she didn't really have much emotional comfort to offer me. I'm sure she was scared to death. Her breadwinner, and husband, now-father, had fallen ill with something that couldn't be measured very well, or medicated very well, or planned for or predicted. Though I couldn't understand it at the time, due to my myopic narcissism, I can now see how difficult her road was with me. I honor the fantastic work she did as a parent to our two children and in keeping our boat afloat during some emotionally wracking times.

But my then-wife wasn't really all that emotionally available. Even when things were good, she didn't express a lot of emotion. She was much more logical and calculated. We had a good mix together when things were good, emotional and logical. But when things got sparse or challenging, we often went to our respective corners and sulked.

I didn't know about Gary Chapman's **Love Languages** at that time. We tried a lot of soul-searching. We did therapy together and by ourselves. We worked at it. I DO absolutely believe that she gave it everything she had. In the end, however, things became overwhelming for her, to the point of wanting to leave the marriage and pull the family apart. I still remember being at the last couple's therapy session and us both stating our final assessment of the situation. We were ending our therapy and saying our goodbyes to our therapist and giving in to the dissolution of our marriage.

My then-wife said she did not see things improving. She felt it was better that we divorce. I said I really felt we were at a launching point in our relationship and that we had been given this crisis as a way to express and work through all the things that had fallen apart in our marriage. I wanted to continue. She did not.

I learned that one person cannot keep a marriage together no matter how hard they try or how much they want to keep the family together. I was in agreement that things could not continue as they had been. But I was also convinced that she was still the woman I was in love with, and that the marriage was stronger than our current complaints or disagreements.

But, of course, I couldn't make her want to work it out with me.

Okay, so it wasn't all about depression and emotional availability. We both worked hard at being in the relationship and being good parents to our two children. But along the way, we fell into unhealthy coping mechanisms that drove us apart rather than together.

Today, I can say, I have been seen at my worst, by a new woman, after the divorce, and she embraced me through it. And as I was thrashing in my own bile, I gained a perspective at some point that went like this. "What about her experience of this mess? She's going through this, too. I have to give some credence to her strength and love for me and step up, even for today (if that's the best I can manage), to support her experience of this relationship and our time together."

For a moment I was able to get out of my own self-pity and self-destruction and say, "Wait, what about her experience?"

It was a bit of a zen moment. To be so deep in a depression that everything in the world seems dark, and yet to rise above it and try and take her wants and desires into consideration. It was like an out-of-body experience. I looked down at my sad self and at her happy (maybe shaken) self and asked, "What does she want this relationship to look like? What about *her* experience of happiness at this moment?"

And it was indeed this little fulcrum that allowed me to crack the black heavy cloak that was shrouding out all light. And add into the equation our deep physical bond and commitment to staying close. As I gave back to her, tried to stay open and communicative, she showed me she was not afraid. By staying close, she affirmed her own words, "I'm going to stick around."

To have an ally and a lover who can take me in ON and OFF mode. What a blessing she is.

Divorcing With Kids: The Golden Rule - It's About Time, Not Money

John McElhenney

Time is the number one parenting resource.

Divorce was the biggest disruption and reset of my entire life. Because we had kids, I knew the way we handled the separation and business of divorce was going to be of critical importance to them. My dad's departure from the scene changed everything about my life.

I remember the moment I learned that my then-wife had been to consult with an attorney. I called my long-time mentor and sometimes-therapist and asked how soon he could see me. Within hours I was in his office sobbing. It was clear as I began talking about what was happening that I was grieving as a seven-year-old boy. I was crying for the sadness inside me that was really about *my* parents' divorce. I could still feel the broken heart as if I were reliving it.

My concern going into the divorce was how to protect my kids from experiencing the disruption that had blown through all of my childhood family dreams. Later that evening I argued with my then-wife about her request that I simply leave the house. "We can tell them you're going on a business trip, or something," she'd said, earlier in the therapy. She said she needed a break from the intensity.

It was April. Our kids were in third and fifth grade, two months from completing the school year. I flat-out refused. Even as the therapist was telling us he thought we could use some time apart, I disagreed.

"The divorce is going to take a while to figure out," I demanded. "We've been living as roommates for some time. We can make another seven weeks until school is out. I'm not disrupting their school year because you want a break."

It was a very hard close of the school year, but I am proud I stuck to my guns and stayed in the house. Sure, my kids were aware that things weren't great, but they didn't have the ground torn out from underneath them, either.

As we went into the negotiations around separating our two lives, we did a good job keeping the "best interest of the kids" ahead of our own. We paid money to an expensive and fantastic therapist who made her living helping couples build amicable parenting plans to guide the next five to ten years of their kids' lives. We paid to meet with a divorce accountant who modeled the various scenarios. (She keeps the house. You keep the house. You sell the house.) We did everything right, as far as we could tell.

In this process, I was grieving as we went along. I even caused a pause in the process when the parenting-plan therapist learned that I didn't want to go through with the divorce. We took an extra week and a few sessions to see what that might look like, if we didn't get a divorce. I was trusting in the team we had hired and in my still-wife's good intentions towards the kids. Everything was about the kids.

Even though a lot of the divorce process is about money, the focus should really be on the time. As I was trying to be the compliant good dad, good guy, good divorcing man, I began to compromise on some of the items I had brought to the negotiations. While my then-wife was focused and clear on her desires (custodial parent, house, child support), I was a bit disoriented. My only expressed desire was 50/50 custody and 50/50 parenting.

The problem was, even the cooperative therapist began to tell me I should settle for what she wanted. At that time, in the state of Texas, she was accurate when she said, "That's what she will get if you go to court. She knows that. So let's just start with things we can negotiate."

Even as I was clear and determined to have a low-conflict divorce, and to get as much time as possible with my kids, I was a bit misled by our counselor. It was 50% of my money that we were paying her to stay out of the courts. And she quickly sold me into the bad deal that is offered as the typical divorce in Texas (and likely in your state). The SPO becomes the law of the land. In our case, I was asked to accept that very unbalanced arrangement so we could move on to the schedule and the money.

The money will come and bite you in the butt if you don't pay attention, but it was the kids and time with the kids that I was most interested in. Yet within a few weeks my 50/50 schedule ideas were tossed out.

Now, years later, I can tell you this: If you want 50/50 parenting, go for it. Sure, you may have the odds against you, depending on your state and your case, but if that's how you parented, I think that's how you should parent after divorce. The old concept that the mom is more essential to keeping the kids happy simply doesn't hold true. The attorney I talked to recently about renegotiating my divorce arrangement said, "If you go in looking for 50/50 parenting and have some reasonable evidence to support your ability to parent, we're liable to win."

The tides have shifted somewhat. I believe you will most likely be offered the simple deal. For some more traditional marriages, the non-custodial/custodial parent plan works. But for the dads who are 100% into their role as DAD as well as their role as breadwinner, I believe the effort well worth it.

I lost over 65% of my kid-time because I was "given" the SPO and the non-custodial parent role. I also ended up paying more than I should have, because the theoretical job didn't materialize to support the decree. By that time, the only option was to sue my ex-wife for a different arrangement or different financial terms.

1. I didn't have the money to fight.
2. I didn't want to sue anyone, much less the mother of my kids.

You may, in fact, have to sue to get what you want. But if what you want is to be present with your kids as much as possible, you should go for it. I didn't have the choice, based on the people I put trust in and the system that was set up years ago in favor of the mother. With hindsight today, if I knew how much I was giving up, I would have fought for the TIME. The money, even as unbalanced as it was, was less of an issue.

If you put your kids first, you may need to fight to get what you want. And by putting your kids first, sometimes you may have to fight their mom. But to be the best dad you can be, you have to be there, you have to spend time with your kids. All of that time that was taken away is now water under the bridge, but today it's much more clear for me. I take every offer to have the kids an extra night or to support my ex when she has to work late.

Time is the number one parenting resource.

Stay positive. Love your kids. Respect your ex.

John McElhenney

You've heard the metaphor of "the elephant in the room," right? This a little tale about the dinosaur in the divorce. While I work to keep every post on this blog tilted in the positive direction, there have been moments in my relationship to the mother of my children that have been less than stellar.

My ex-wife got mad one summers and threatened me when I got late on my child support payments. I had just lost a job and was in the process of replacing my income, but it was hard times. I'm sure it was hard times on her side of the equation too, and so I try and give her the benefit of the doubt every time. Even when things were bleak between us, I tried to forgive and move on, just as she was trying to convince herself that I would make good on my promise of payments.

After a few months of job hunting, I had not produced a new stream of income for us to base our shared parenting financial obligations, so in a fit of rage or an act of self-preservation, she filed our divorce decree with the attorney general (AG) office in our great state of Texas. In effect, she was throwing up her hands and saying she was tired of hearing my unfulfilled promises of payment; she'd rather have the state's attorneys take over the matter of the cash flow. She used the terms "enforcement" and "in the best interests of the kids" a lot. Actually, she still uses those concepts today, with different language. She's still pretty sure the AG's office is the only reason she's gotten paid recently.

I had to remind her, "Um, the reason you've been getting paid since November is that I had a job. No cash flow, no money for either of us." She didn't like that answer then and she doesn't like the logic today. Still, we have our divorce decree and we have the AG's office tracking my every move.

The bad part about her inviting the AG's office into our financial affairs is that it really doesn't coerce me into paying more or faster. Sorry, I've never defaulted or delayed a payment when I had the money. I even exhausted my retirement account to make payments when my income was not matching my expenses.

It really doesn't matter now, as it stands we have the AG's office in bed with us, for better or for worse, for richer or for poorer, until both our kids are 18 years old.

Today I met with my family attorney and he said, "The AG's office is like a dinosaur. Once you invite the big beast into your affairs, it's really hard to get rid of them." I liked the analogy. Yes, that's what it feels like sometimes, like a great big stegosaurus is sitting on my chest with a dumb smile and a "feed the children" necklace on.

Truth is, my kids have never gone wanting for anything. My ex-wife has never missed a house payment. And my commitment to pay and continued efforts to do so have never wavered. Well, except for that one summer. When she began to rattle her AG saber at me, I pushed back with the only idea I could come up with. I told her (this was a dumb idea) that if she "did in fact file with the AG's office," I would ask for a recalculation of all that I have paid, and all that I should've paid, based on *actual* income rather than *theoretical* (which I had yet to achieve since the divorce). I had agreed to pay child support based on a job that I no longer had, but under the duress of the process I agreed, even before I had the replacement job. Another bad idea.

A few rules in dealing with your co-parent:

1. Never threaten your ex about anything.
2. Remain optimistic, but don't count on a job, or a miracle, or mercy from your ex when they are angry or under stress.
3. If it's in the decree, you will continue owing the amount until you sue your ex to change the amount of child support. Regardless of your employment status, or the economic climate, your child support bills continue to arrive, and your debt, if you can't pay, will continue to grow.
4. Once in your lives, the AG's office will never leave.

Today, my attorney went on with the metaphor. "And getting the dinosaur to change or do something on your behalf is very hard. You can push, yell, ask, write letters, and it's very likely that if the dinosaur moves at all, it will be because of some random reason and not as a result of your request."

He continued, "The AG's office is really run by computer programs. When the computer kicks your name and account out because you are behind on your payments, the staff just sends out the letter. What we want to avoid is getting the dinosaur mad. If you keep paying what you can and keep paying something, when the computer spits out your name, the dinosaur will consider you a friend and not just bite your head off."

"Your ex-wife on the other hand, might have other ideas. But the dinosaur is equally hard to push from her side as well. You are both just kind of stuck with it, like herpes. Once you have the dinosaur in your divorce, you can never completely get rid of him."

The good news in my case was I got a new job. I'd been paying her 25% of my income since my last corporate job, but it never quite equaled the *theoretical* job that I was supposed to land in the first few months after the decree was signed. I dutifully would contact the AG's office, and they dutifully would withhold the child support payments from my take-home pay.

A few things I didn't know about this process.

1. Your ex does not pay taxes on any of the child support income. It's like free money to them. You, however, pay the taxes and lose the money at the same time. (Makes it really seem like a double whammy. I work, I pay taxes, then I give her $1,350.)

2. The AG's office will set an additional payment, on top of your support payment, when you are behind. I called to tell them, "I'm just getting back on my feet, can we reduce the extra payments just a little?" I was told in no uncertain terms, by one of the dinosaur's minions, that I could file a petition to change the support order. So I'd have to sue her? Okay, pass.

3. The dinosaur randomly sends out letters to beneficiaries and asks, "Would you like us to review your account?" Like a bill collector, on their side, the simple checkmark in a box on a return postcard sets all kinds of painful examinations in motion.

I'm lucky. I have been employed or working under contract for most of the time since the divorce. I was gearing up to start a new job so that I could get some money, but more importantly so that my kids would get some money. And yes, the dinosaur would be fed and happy in the next month.

One of my main goals is to keep the dinosaur from kicking out a random request to put me in jail. But according to my attorney, we'd hear the roar via at least one letter of intent before the patrolmen showed up at my door.

Always, no matter what, put your children's lives ahead of the emotional issues you may still have with your co-parent.

Section 5: Freefall and Depression

It is not uncommon for both parents to experience periods of depression following a divorce. As many of your life values become untethered from the daily activity of being a parent, you have to seek and find a new way to find meaning while you are alone. Dads may be displaced by having to leave the home and find new lodgings. And in my case, I had to move in with my sister because my job had ended just before my then-wife asked for a divorce.

Minimizing the Collateral Damage of Depression and Divorce

John McElhenney

Why is it that when I'm depressed I cannot see the hope in the pattern? Why do I sink so far that even my own internal dialogue is powerless to lift my spirits? It's not like I haven't been depressed before. It's not like I don't know that I eventually rise back out of my funk. But somewhere in the short-circuit of my brain, I can no longer experience joy or hope.

The hope is a real killer. It's this vicious and toxic self-talk that I moderate by getting completely quiet. Sure, it's not a good sign when I'm no longer my boisterous self, but it's also safer for me not to be spouting off my doomsday fantasies.

I can see that these thoughts are flawed. I can even state to myself, "Man, you are really hitting some f-ed up thinking here. Let's not pay too much attention to this storm." But I always DO pay too much attention to it. Or I consume so much of my own energy battling the wicked thoughts that I begin to shut off from everyone around me.

As a parent dealing with depression, I've had to substantially moderate my communications with my kids and ex-wife during these periods. Several years ago when I was going through some of the upheavals of the divorce, I had a pretty open conversation with my kids about my "cloud." My son came to the rescue. "You mean like that commercial where the cloud follows the guy around raining on him? Like that?"

This is the only time a pharma-porn ad for an antidepressant has ever served a purpose in my life, other than reminding me that I'm depressed. My son really understood the concept, and the cartoon illustrations seemed to make the disease more manageable.

And as we progressed through that difficult summer, my son would occasionally ask, "How's your cloud today?"

It was a great opening. I was able to reassure both of my kids that my difficulties had nothing to do with them. And that I was working with a doctor and some cloud-removal medicine of my own. It was a nice bridge for us to be able to chat about Dad's issues. And when kids reach the age where onset depression might arise, I'm so glad we have the framework to talk about things like medication and the state of my cloud.

Even my ex-wife is supportive these days when things are "off." She notices when my email responses take days rather than hours. It's not her fault that she needs help and has questions we have to answer together as parents. My depression does not abide by our needs or our schedule. And this year she texted me, "Are you having a hard time this Christmas?" Yep, as painful as it was to admit to her, it was more painful to hide the truth.

So I struggle with depression from time to time. Most of the time the onset has something to do with earning a living and the joy or panic around my employment. And today, I'm with a person who can embrace all of my flavors, and while she's not enthusiastic about my quietudes, she is very clear that she is sticking with me, through thick and thin. She's much better at the thin times then I am.

So moving forward, my challenge is to understand that cycle. Is it bipolar? I don't know, I think Bradley Cooper in *Silver Lining Playbook* did us all a service by demonstrating the warped highs and lows of that variation of depression, but I'm not sure it's that helpful a diagnosis. See, when I'm down my entire life suffers. When I'm UP, or HAPPY, or ENTHUSIASTIC, my life feels and looks as if everything is going well.

Well, what if the UPSIDE is merely my life going well? I have not spun off in a manic mode (out of control euphoria) since I did drugs in my high school days. My "highs" these days are really what I consider my full, creative, and activated self. Does this mean I'm cycling UP? Or that I'm getting hypo-manic? (Hypo, meaning just below the destructive mania.) I don't think so. My meds doctor is not all that convinced that the label is very helpful in treating me.

So I get LOW. Those are the times I need the most help. When I'm UP I'm usually plugging along quite nicely. That's the person I feel I really am. The UP person expresses himself in music, writing, and singing.

The LOW part I have to work to repair. I do not need to jettison everything in my life when I start having a LOW period. I need to hold on to the tiny hopes:

1. My mate will stand beside me through the storm.
2. The storm will pass.
3. Joy will return to my life.

As we move forward as a family, I am certain I will have difficult times again. But now I'm going to counsel myself and encourage my family to reflect back to me, with this truth: the LOW passes. If I can work to reduce collateral damage while I'm suffering from this brain flu, I will do everyone, including myself, a favor.

So that's it. The hope is in the future moderation and mitigation of the LOW. To deny that it will happen again, or get overly cocky and optimistic about my happy times, is to open myself to the blind spot that is my depression.

But the message I need to keep repeating, even in the good times, is THE JOY WILL RETURN. If I can leverage that into some measure of hopefulness, then I am well along my path of recovery. I don't have to aim for joy when I am activated and functioning properly. I do need to remember before, during, and after my LOW that I recover. I return fully and joyfully to my life. Forever and ever, amen.

A Good Man in a Storm, Even After Divorce

John McElhenney

The irony here is often the storm is me. I'm sorry about that, my depression and I can cause a few problems. But for the most part, about 85% of the time when things are tough and about 95% of the time when things are good, I'm an excellent companion come rain or shine. It's the rain times that broke apart my marriage.

It wasn't for lack of trying. We tried. We survived. We worked through enormous hurdles and came out of the trials and tribulations with two beautiful and blessed kids.

But the hardships were unbelievably hard. In my mind that gave us even MORE staying power through the down times. But for my then-wife, something must've broken at some point. She no longer believed in the promise of our marriage, and she decided to take her chances, and unfortunately the chances for the rest of us, with other options. Divorce options.

It was sort of sprung on me, even though we'd be in couples therapy on and off for several years. You can't say we didn't work it. We were doing the best we could. And we did pretty damn good through the hospital times with our second child. And we did okay in the times when my depression debilitated me for about a year. (I can explain this later, but not excuse it.)

So we'd been going to therapy, not to fix our relationship, specifically, but to help us learn how to communicate better. To stay in the reality of the situation rather than our own projections of what we "thought" was going on. Systems-Centered Therapy (SCT), it was called.

And that aspect of our therapist was grand. He really was helping us break down our own fears and misperceptions and get back to what was actually real, what the other person had intended to say, rather than what we heard. He let us know he was not a couples therapist. He was helping us get centered and clear with one another. And maybe that was exactly what he did.

The problem with SCT, however, is it does not really deal with emotions about the realities. It simply redirects you to what you know and what you are projecting about the future or lamenting about the past. We spend, as humans, a lot of time OUT of the present moment. And that's a problem. So Rich wasn't trying to fix us or fix our marriage, he was trying to get us to tell the other person what we really wanted. What was really bothering us. And keep it 100% real.

Now, it seems to me that this would have been the perfect venue for my still-wife to tell me she was considering life without me, BEFORE going to consult with an attorney. But she didn't do it that way. I found out in REALITY THERAPY that she'd already been to see a lawyer. Then when the emotions flooded forward from my disbelief and shock, our therapist sort of fell short of the mark. He consciously didn't jump in the middle of it. Well, actually he did. I'll get to that in a minute.

When my then-wife said exactly what she felt was her truth, it was actually a projection about the future. So in that aspect, the therapist should've redirected her back to this moment and what was real. He did not.

Here's what she ultimately said, "You have a very hard time with honesty. And I don't trust that things are going to get better. And I don't have hope for the future of this marriage."

Here's what I was saying about my reality. "Things have been hard. We've done great at working through hardships that have been thrown at us. And at this moment in time, I have MORE hope that our future is as bright as it's ever been. Even this therapy is stripping away our worries and helping us focus on what is real."

But it wasn't enough to convince her to stay with me. And I was devastated right there in our little "emotion-free" therapy session. Rich allowed her to stay in her projected reality and also took her side when she asked that I simply walk out of the house that night and tell the kids I was off on a business trip.

Again, bullshit, and again a failing of our therapist who should've been helping us communicate rather than siding with one of us. He agreed that she was under such stress that she needed some time off. Some time to recover her center.

"Why doesn't she leave the house, then?" I asked, point-blank.

Neither of them supported that idea. I'm not exactly sure why. And I fought with both of them, again. Not really the right role for an SCT therapist, but that's what really happened. He was convinced I should leave her and the kids alone for a bit and regroup to see if there was something to salvage. I was in my own reality that THIS WAS THE EXACT TIME TO STAY REAL rather than lie to the kids and run out the door.

So I stood and fought. And we went to two more sessions with Rich, more for closure then progression. At this point, he retreated back into SCT and the reality of the situation. The last session was more of an apology between the three of us for not being able to save the marriage. We were saying goodbye to each other and to Rich as our enabler.

I'm not sure I would've gotten better results from a Gottisman couples therapist. I'm not sure I really needed to stay in that marriage. Sure, I can say I'm sad about all the kid-years of time I lost to her rash decision and our therapist's inability to keep himself out of our business, but in the end, today, I'd have to say it was a good thing.

You see, some people have different happy set-points. And I think hers is different than mine. A ton of things could make her unhappy. And often she found (still finds) ways to make it about me. How I'm not taking care of her in the right way.

Again, SCT would direct her back to the reality of the situation.

1. You are unhappy.
2. You think he is causing you to be unhappy.
3. But the unhappiness is in your thinking and not in his actions. He is not preventing you from changing the situation if it gets that bad.
4. You can change your thinking at any time.
5. The house is not too messy. The house is more messy than you would like it. It's not his responsibility to clean the house until you feel better. That's why you hired a maid.
6. You're too focused on what he's doing or not doing. Focus on yourself.

Those are some pretty good words of advice for any relationship. Oh and this one: If you're not having sex with each other, and the disconnect goes on for months at a time, something is out of whack. Even an SCT therapist should key in on this REALITY. But he didn't.

I hope the best for my ex-wife and the mother of my two kids. I see now that with her new man, she's still about the same. She's not all that happy. He's probably not doing exactly what she would like either. But that's the real lesson here. In relationships, people need to look after their own realities and the ways those realities intersect with another's reality.

In the case of my then-wife, she was unhappy about many things. I was happy about many things. It seems to me today we're pretty much in the same situation, we're just no longer married, and some real complications have entered our court. She's pretty convinced that I'm not supporting her correctly. The good part is I am no longer answering to her happiness, I no longer need to do her chores. That was about her. And perhaps more about her lack of desire for sex.

It was a reality I could not manage. In the end, it was a reality that should've split us up and did. I am now free to have a relationship with a woman who enjoys life, who wakes up laughing, like I do. Sure, she's got a list of things she'd like me to do differently, and I'm sure I have a few items for her. BUT we're here by choice. WE love each other, daily, by choice. We don't even have kids between us. But we love, laugh, and let go.

Love. Laugh. Let go. That's a much better fit. So, in the end, I guess I'm grateful to both Rich and my ex-wife for releasing me for the next phase of my life.

LOVE.
LAUGH.
LET GO.

Losing Everything Again, And Finding Happiness Anyway

John McElhenney

I'm in a rough place. At the same time, I can't say that I've ever been happier. But I'm just beginning to realize happiness is about my relationship with myself and not someone else. Sure, I'd like to be in a relationship. I really miss the physical contact, the camaraderie, the checking-in at all hours of the day with little texts and messages. I love being in love. And I love being in a relationship. Until it's not working. Then I'm not all that good at expressing what I need to make things better. So I suffer. I moan. I get depressed. What I should get is ANGRY. But I suck at that even more.

Two months ago I was asked to move out of "her" house. I was broken. I was freaked out and scared that I was retreating to my mom's house to die. I imagined myself sleeping all the time, fighting with my mom about not getting up, like a teenager. I knew the sadness was going to be overwhelming. I mean, I loved this woman with all my being, and she was everything I dreamed I wanted in a relationship, and now she was going away? I was almost as afraid of the darkness I was going to descend into, more than the darkness I was in, but I knew that staying was not healthy. I was anxious and depressed at the same time. And I needed to get out of the house and get on with the grief and healing that would come from losing it all again.

For the first two weeks, I suffered. Very differently than I thought I would. I was sad. I was grieving. But I was also relieved. I relaxed a bit once I was alone again. I slept better. I napped anytime I felt tired. I took back control of my schedule and my priorities. And one thing I did, for sure, was exercise every day. It was a commitment I'd made over a year ago when I was struggling. No matter what, I can walk. Even if it's only three miles or so. I can walk. And while it might not make me feel better in the short term, in the long run I knew it was as good for my soul as it was for my health.

I also attended a boatload of Al-Anon meetings. I was going almost to keep from being so alone. But I was listening too. And I spoke a few times about the struggle of giving up on a relationship. I got a lot of phone numbers of people I could call when I just needed someone to talk to. It was the best support network I could've asked for. These people had experience with what I was going through. Most of them had years in the program and gave pretty sage advice when asked for it. But mainly they were sounding boards for my recovery thinking, about the relationship, about where I was going, about how sad I was, about how I couldn't see my future at all. Mostly they listened. That's really what we need more than anything, someone to listen.

Well, as it turns out, I never really fell apart. I was expecting it to happen at any time, but I simply kept going on with my life. I kept walking. I read and worked the Al-Anon program. I went to meetings. I talked to some people on the phone. I got a sponsor. And I really just struggled on with my normal life, except that I was alone and not living with someone. (Well, my mom, but that is different. And we worked out a pretty good relationship around privacy and sharing resources.)

I sought out the grief. I watched sad movies and cried. I read books about breaking up and grieving. I wrote goodbye letters to my former fiancé. I dug into my feelings and sat there, not really sure what actions to take. So I stayed still. I sat with the feelings. I prayed and meditated. I ate three meals a day and walked in the brutal Texas heat. And I kept going.

I wasn't feeling better during those first few weeks. I was feeling liberated, somehow, but sad and alone.

About three weeks in, something happened. (I think my new meds kicked in.) I started to see possibilities for the future, my future, alone but surviving. If you've never experienced true depression, you don't quite understand the depth of the helplessness that happens. I didn't really see my demise, I just couldn't imagine my survival. But a new dawn began to break as a result of my work, my time away from a toxic relationship, and the help of my chemical-altering drugs.

At about four weeks, my brain kicked back in. It was as if I had been sleeping the entire time prior, and now awake I was capable of accomplishing anything. I wasn't grandiose, I was just happy again. I was hopeful again. I was still doing all the same things, walking, napping, getting plenty of sleep, eating well, and boom, like a light switch was flipped, I was back.

That was six weeks ago and the reignition has stuck. I've gotten over the edgy side effects of the new meds. I've calmed down my fantastic ideas. I've watched my sleep schedule very carefully. And I'm still soaring what I consider my "normal" functioning self. I'm happy. I'm alone and living at my mother's house and working a shit job, but I'm happy. And I'm writing. That's one of the big tells with me; if I stop writing, something is off. My brain likes to express itself with language. When I clam up, I'm battling something bigger than just a temporary setback or disappointment.

I've learned to ride the edge of my good feelings too. And I've learned to laugh off the overused term "manic." Sure, back in my teen years I had a manic phase. But since then, when I get high, I think I'm returning to my natural "high self." There are psychological terms for this state as well, but I don't even think hypo-manic fits for me. I could get there if I drank too much coffee, didn't eat well, and didn't watch my sleep. I could easily slip over the edge of mania and do some crazy shit. But I learned when I was sixteen that this type of behavior only results in sadness later.

So I'm alone, homeless, and happy. How joyful I will be as things begin to turn in my favor. And it's the season, fall, when I usually get stronger. I'm trying to relax a bit more. I'm thrashing a bit about being alone. But at the moment, as you can imagine, I don't have many options for being in a relationship. And I KNOW that I don't need another relationship right now. My relationship to myself is the one I need to nurture and continue to build. I've still got a lot of forgiving to do for my failures and failings. At the moment, though, I am well on my way.

Divorce Lessons: It's the Quiet Time, the Alone Time, the Empty Spaces

John McElhenney

When you're happily married you think life is all set. Then you have kids, and the world gets even bigger and brighter. Then some tough times come along and muck up the happily ever after. And after much hand-wringing, and arguments the money is settled, the housing is decided upon, and Dad (that's me) is out on his own, to fend for himself, in the world of being a single dad with normal custody, that is to say, about 30%.

Some days I roll along like a happy man, a single dad working the program, doing his best. Other days, I fall below the "joy" quotient and would really rather chill in my bed, watch movies, surf the net, and withdraw from all the activity. The holidays are some of the hardest times, for some reason. And today, when I delivered my kids to my old house, my wife's house, I was a bit bereft. Lonely. Aimless. Sad.

It's not that anything specific happened. In fact, just the opposite. My life is feeling pretty sweet, considering. But today, as I was getting back in my car, backing out of my old driveway, with no particular place to go, I felt the punch. A light poke in the solar plexus. A minor ache that continued to echo through my body the rest of the afternoon. It's the little things that get you.

Like little places you pass that remind you of a good moment. And we had a lot of good moments before we had all the bad moments. Today, eating lunch, I pulled into a place, not on purpose, that was one of the last good times I remember with my ex. She was working nearby, and we had made plans to meet for lunch. It was in the golden moment, right after I'd had my vasectomy when we were trying to score the 40 ejaculates before we could have the well-earned unprotected sex. For a month, my wife rediscovered her libido or something. She joked that it was more about hitting the goal. I was thrilled for the renewal and imagined the sex ahead would be even better.

After a divorce, you count back in your head, sometimes, the moments when you knew things were great and the moments when you first sensed that things were spiraling out of control, in the wrong direction. The little moments of magic can pop up, like today, and trigger the old hurt. And who, knows, maybe there was part of me that wanted to lean into the ache that was already taking root in my chest.

This last moment flashed before me today, as I was eating at this funky little Mexican restaurant, and there was a pang of sadness, a worry, will I ever have another moment, another love so good? The moment strikes at the heart of what ultimately blew us apart, and so this little scene of playful joy is not important, except for the feeling I still get when I remember it. We were happy, joyful in our quest for liberated sex again...

In tje good old days, this one time, we met at this restaurant, and in the parking lot around to the side, my wife gave me a quickie blow job, in the silliest and playful way. We were like kids, getting away with something terribly forbidden. Today, the flicker of that moment showed two people playing at sex, enjoying the raucous play, and getting away with a little secret in the middle of the workday.

I guess the deeper part of the ache is the lack of spontaneous or playful sex I've had in the years since that peak. When the condoms came off, the sex continued at ever slowing pace. It seems the "goal" really was part of the fun for my then-wife. I tried to rekindle whatever I could from my end, but things continued to fade. She became less willing to even be close, much less have sex.

Sex is not everything, but it's important. As our sex life continued to fade, I continued to be the interested party who was given the challenge to "ask differently" and "keep the house clean" and "pay all the bills." It was as if there were a string of conditions for intimacy that became more of an alchemical mixture than anything I could predict or influence. Why is it, that this stereotype is so common? Men continue to want sex. Women, as we now know, get bored within monogamous relationships. Um, no shit. Men do, too. Everyone has to be willing to work on the monotony with more intention.

In the last year of my marriage, I am certain we could easily go for a month at a stretch without having sex. And it's not that I wasn't asking, cajoling, seeing if she wanted a massage. Her switch flipped off and stayed off. There was not much I could do about it. As I was making lists of things I could do to entice her, she was becoming more distant.

In a recent post by a friend, on **what to get your husband for Christmas**, I was saddened that the tone, even from this psychologist, was so one-sided. Here's the list.

1. Oral Sex
2. Regular Sex
3. Some Other Sexual Thing…
4. Appreciation
5. Love
6. Wear a Santa Hat and Nothing Else

This is a common theme. The "how sex used to be" theme. In a Facebook post, this therapist poses a theoretical question from a reader.

> "Why his wife last 69ed before they had kids, 12 years ago. Then i can answer, with solemnity:
> My friend, there is probably no amount of doing the chores that is going to get you that again. It's one of those things that women only do when they are young and uninhibited, like dyeing their hair purple, or dancing on top of the bar.
> Now if you took care of the kids for an entire weekend while she visited the friend with whom she used to dye her hair purple and dance on top of the bar….. then maybe.
> No promises."

But that's the point. I was doing the extra things. I was offering her "girl's night out." I was taking care of putting the kids to bed so she could get in the mood. Except, more often than not, she was falling asleep or working on a project when I came out of the kid's room.

We all have to work on our sexual communication. If it gets off, we need to chat about it. If it REALLY gets off, we need to bring it front-and-center in therapy. Somehow I was letting our sexual disconnect be "okay." We went to therapy, but we were usually dealing with some "crisis" that I didn't really see as a crisis. And I'm sure that was the problem. I wanted closeness, and maybe even sex. She wanted all the worries and struggles of the day to be gone.

Sure, men have an easier time getting turned on, and women take some warming up. But women also have to be open to suggestion or it's a non-starter, no matter how you phrase it or what technique you use to rub her feet. Needless to say, it wasn't the sex that caused us to get a divorce, but the loss of sexual connection sure indicated that something had gotten out of balance. Unfortunately, I was never able to regain that balance with my then-wife. And as the emotional aspects of our relationship got more complicated, the sex simply dried up completely.

So, dear therapist, what is a man in a committed relationship, who *is* doing all the extra things and still getting the cold shoulder, supposed to do? Move on?

Section 6: Loss Is Part of the Journey

Everyone loses in divorce. The kids lose their full-time loving parents working as a team. Each parent loses a significant amount of time with their kids. And everyone in the family has to make peace with what has happened, even if they don't know why it happened. It is from the loss that we are forced to rebuild ourselves into something new and more resilient.

John McElhenney

Happy 12th birthday, my sweet daughter. I hope you got my texts and voicemail.

I'm sorry I couldn't be with you on your special day, but we'll catch up on Thursday.

And while I know you won't understand this now, at some point in the future, I want you to know I'm sorry for all of the misses and all the ways I have not been able to be there for you. But I have not been away from you by choice. I did not miss your birthdays, as much as miss you overall. Out of sight, I'm guessing, is out of mind in your world, and that's as it should be. But we shouldn't be apart so much.

Today, on your birthday, I thought about you all the time. And some of the times I texted you funny "dad" texts. I tried to blow up your phone during lunch. (Yes, I know when you have lunch, every day.) I wanted the smile on your face to be from me as I celebrated this wonderful day (with) for you. I want to show up in your life as much as I can.

As I walked through your room this morning, I felt your absence. I noticed the lack of your messy pile of clothes, I noticed the clean and steam-free bathroom, I noticed the made bed. You see, I notice when you are gone. And I can tell sometimes, when we are together, that you too are longing for more time. So let's make the most of what we do have.

I know you are growing up. I can see it every time we're together. I am fascinated by the few stories I get in the blur of dinner, homework, and school night bedtimes. I love how your sense of humor is reflecting some of my wackiness. I love how you tell stories with excitement and a great punchline. You're a natural.

As you go on towards your teens, you're going to start detaching even more from me and your mom, it's part of growing up. And even as I know it's coming, I feel like the process began 4.5 years ago, when your mom and I told you we were getting a divorce. It was one of the hardest days of my life. I kept the brave face and so did you. In that moment of shell shock, you were the first to speak. "Which pets are you going to take?"

It was one of your shining moments. As you leaped from the crisis to the practical matter at hand, cats and dogs. And we could reassure you that the pets weren't going anywhere, only me. Only your dad, who wouldn't be moving back into the house.

I want everything for you. I want to be smothering and I want to be strong and stoic. I want to show you how a good man should treat you, talk to you, open doors for you. I want to keep your heart soft and open by teaching you how to listen for truth and intention. I want to protect you in every storm you will encounter, but I won't be there in person to do it.

As you pull away from both of us, your mom and me, during the next years of your wonderful life, I want to give you a piece of my love that will never fade. I want you to know how much I love you, in spite of leaving you alone. I want to give you the confidence that I will never judge or deny you. I want to be the red emergency phone that you can call without hesitation when things don't go the way you planned. I want to be your dad, the best dad I can be. Even from here, I am reaching out daily to hold you, and I know you can't feel it. But you will. Eventually, you will separate from both of us and you will find the love that has been given to you, for your entire life. My steadfast love has never wavered.

Walk on, my sweet daughter. Walk on with the confidence that comes from having a solid father in your life. And even as we have fewer days and hours together, know that I am always here, just on the other side of the text or the phone call.

Transformational Divorce

John McElhenney

My entire world (kids, wife, house, work, neighborhood, sports, money, creative life, play) exploded into tiny pieces. When the business of divorce had been done, I got what 90% of divorcing dads in America get: 35% of the time with their kids, the non-custodial parent role, a big child support obligation, and no house. It's as if I went from Pleasantville to homeless in a matter of weeks. And the homelessness is no joke. The financial and psychological drains on a father in the midst of divorce are immense. I was barely able to stay afloat. And more than once I wondered if I was going to be able to stay alive. Perhaps my large life insurance policy would be better for my kids than me. WOW.

I've been working on selling my "Whole Parent" story as The Positive Divorce, but maybe that's too tame. What happened after my divorce was life-altering for me, my ex-wife, and my kids. And the Phoenix from the Flames has been my creative power that caught fire. My writing found a deeper voice and my blog audience began to grow. I wouldn't have wished for it, but I now see, looking back, that my divorce was the best thing that ever happened to me.

Sure we were making the best of it, but we weren't happy. We had very different ideas about what the other person "should" be doing. I liked my kids, I liked my job (except when I hated it) and I did my best to support my loving and beautiful wife through every aspect of our relationship. But something was always wrong. Something never met her expectations. I couldn't figure it out, but I learned that I couldn't fix it, either.

Lesson #1 before the transformation: I could not make her happy. I could not fix her. I could only keep myself focused on myself. (An old Al-Anon concept: never take another person's inventory. You can only manage your own.)

Lesson #2 before the transformation: I am responsible for my happiness and the support and caring of those around me. But no one else can make me happy. If I struggled with depression, it was only me who was going to be able to bootstrap my way back to joy.

Lesson #3 before the transformation: Kids are the center of the universe, but kids will not save your marriage or make your life worth living. Kids are a lot of work. The most amazing and rewarding work of all, but still… The stress of having kids really toppled some balance my then-wife had kept together for our entire courtship. She went from happy and self-satisfied to exhausted and angry. That wasn't really the kids, it was a tendency in her that only she could deal with.

Lesson #4 before the transformation: Therapists can be good or bad. A bad therapist can enable and encourage poor behavior. A bad therapist can coddle a depression. A bad therapist may do more damage to your relationship than no therapist. My then-wife had a personal therapist who allowed her to bury her feelings and not deal with issues until they became HUGE. My therapist allowed me to let her go even when I knew it was the hardest thing I would ever do.

Lesson #5 before the transformation: Before the divorce, you have no idea how you are going to survive. The time without your kids. The depression and loneliness. All the darkness of the divorce brought me to my knees. And that's when I learned to pick myself and my needs back up off the floor, dust them off by myself, and put a plan together to get what I wanted next.

Lesson #6 before the transformation: Love seems like a long shot when you are losing the love of your life and your kids. But the transformation will burn away the sorrow at some point. The love you are letting go of will transform into power, direction, and clarity as you reach out for what you really want, now that you know.

Lesson #7 before the transformation: The kids seem to suffer, but they will be okay as well. My two children were five and seven when the transformation happened. Today they are two of the happiest, most well-adjusted teenagers I know. While they know the price we all paid in away time, they seem happy and well-directed in their own lives. While I didn't know if I could survive divorce, I was more worried about my kids.

If you minimize the war with your ex-partner, you can give the kids a hopeful and optimistic outlook on life, even when things don't work out as planned. None of us would've wanted the divorce to happen. But as I talk with my kids today, we all agree that things are better now. I'm happier. Their mom seems to be happier. That's the goal, happier and more centered in life, for all of us.

The transformation took about four years for me. I have mapped it out.

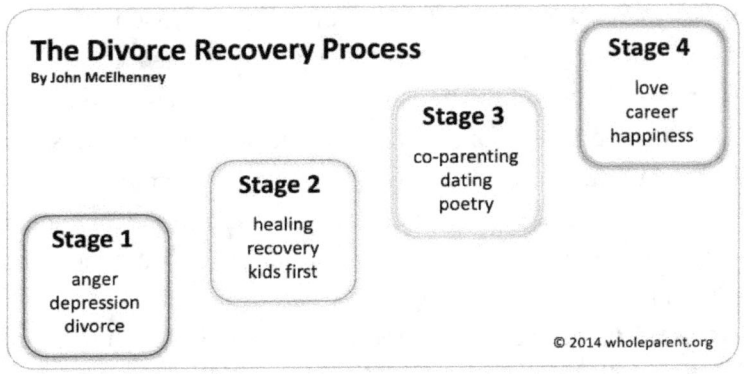

STAGE 1: It's time to let your guard down and grieve. You've just gotten a divorce. Let that sink in. Miss your kids and allow that longing to penetrate your ego. Get angry. Find new things to do with your energy. Find new hobbies and activities.

STAGE 2: As your life stabilizes a little, you begin to refocus your priorities around the kids. Without the marriage as a focus, you can pour your energy into your children. You also will need to begin your own healing process. Start a martial arts class, join a divorce recovery group, begin journaling. It's time to work on YOUR recovery.

STAGE 3: You begin grasping terms like co-parenting. You are now working more as a team. You may not agree with your former spouse, but you can agree on what's best for the kids. As you begin feeling stronger and more yourself, you might begin to date again. Don't start dating too soon, you're liable to end up in another failed relationship.

STAGE 4: As your life begins coming together, you can leave relationships that don't serve your future goals. It's easy to make your kids a priority, but you'd like to have a companion along for the journey. You realize the job is a means to an end, not the meaning of your life. The "off parent" hours are spent doing things you love and perhaps finding another person to love.

In four short years, my life went from shambles to aspirational. I learned that I was not going to settle for half-ass again. I had overlooked some early warning signs at the beginning of our relationship and marriage. I won't make those same mistakes again. After the transformation, you can reset your priorities. You are being given another chance to do it better, to get it right.

My divorce was the transformation I needed in my life to get back on track. I learned what made me happy. I learned I really needed to be with someone who shared the same sense of joy and wonder at the world, that I could wake up with every morning and say thanks to the universe for. I was looking for a "we" that made my life bigger and better. My marriage provided a lot of growth, two wonderful kids, and the transformational experience that reoriented my life completely.

I give thanks to my ex-wife for releasing me back into the universe. I needed to grow and re-find myself and what made me happy. Then I could seek out a more like-minded partner and set up a long-term relationship on mutual goals and mutual adoration.

Bad Daddy and the Delicious Breakfast Dilemma (A Single-Parent Fable)

John McElhenney

"Daddy, will you make me an English muffin?" she asked, waking up just before noon on a summer Tuesday.

"What is hard about making an English muffin?" Daddy asked. "Is something too hard for you?"

"Yes, I want you to make it," said the daughter, Little Lazy Lucy, as she slouched into the comfy chair to pet the cat.

"I see," Daddy said. "Is it too hard to cut the English muffin?"

"Yes, Daddy."

"What about the butter?" Daddy asked. "Do you find that too taxing as well?"

"Yes, Daddy, you do it so much better."

"And adding the jelly," Daddy prodded, "is that part difficult for you in some way?"

"Daddy, please make me a muffin, I'm much to tired to do it."

"And what about eating the English muffin, is that too hard?" he asked.

"No, that part I'm really good at."

"Very well," said Daddy, "I'll start on an English muffin."

And with that Daddy went into the kitchen while LLLucy scrunched even further into the comfy chair and laughed as the cat kneaded into her soft belly.

Upstairs another door flew open and dapper son Badly Buzy Ben announced, "Breakfast? What's for breakfast?" as he stomped down the stairs. His hair was perfectly done and his suit looked freshly pressed. The blue tie matching and shining in concert with his pocket square.

"Daddy," he said, as he entered the room and eyed LLLucy with disdain. "I am hungry."

"Very well, Ben," Daddy said, "What did you have in mind to fix for yourself?"

"Um… What are you making?" he asked, noticing the English muffin Daddy was cutting in half.

"Little Lazy Lucy has asked for an English muffin," Daddy said. "But she's too lazy to help."

"I would like some bacon and eggs," BBBen announced.

"Great," Daddy said, "We've got eggs, but I think we're out of bacon. So you're almost all set. You could put the eggs on an English muffin if you like."

"Will you make my eggs?" BBBen asked.

"Why," Daddy asked. "Is something wrong with your arms and legs?"

"No, Daddy, but I'm in a hurry, and I've got a homework assignment that's due in 15 minutes. Can you make it, please?"

"It only takes about five minutes to scramble some eggs, let me show you where they are," Daddy said.

"I'm really not that hungry," BBBen said, looking quite skinny in his fine suit.

"Yes, I understand," Daddy said. "If you actually grew and filled out, you'd need a whole new wardrobe."

"It's not that, Daddy, I'm just very busy this morning, and I'd prefer your eggs to my own."

"Nicely said," Daddy replied. "I'm pretty sure if you have time to eat the eggs, you have time to make them."

"Okay, I'll just have an apple and go back to my room." He said.

Daddy cut the English muffin and put it into the toaster oven.

The timer was set to dark, but he knew that this really resulted in the perfect toasting of the English muffin.

"Do you want to come put the butter on?" he asked, LLLucy.

"No Daddy, Shadow is kneading my belly and I'd really rather stay here."

"Very well," Daddy said, as he shaved a few pieces of butter onto the steaming English muffin. The smell of toasted muffin and melting butter began to fill the kitchen, and Daddy could feel his own tummy rumble. "This sure smells good," Daddy said. "It's making me hungry."

"I can smell it do, Daddy. It does smell delicious."

"Would you like to come put the strawberry jelly on the muffin?" Daddy asked.

"Can you do it, Daddy, I'm much too relaxed here with Shadow," she said. The cat had curled up in her lap and was licking his paws vigorously. It was a nice scene. Daddy could understand how it was hard to get up when getting up meant upsetting the cat in your lap. So he proceeded to put the organic strawberry preserves on the warm and buttery English muffin.

"Yum, Daddy. That smells great. Is it almost ready?" LLLucy asked.

Daddy didn't answer.

"Daddy? Is my English muffin ready?"

Daddy walked out the front door with the English muffin in hand. "Yes, the English muffin is delicious and ready, but it's not yours. I made it."

"Daaaady," LLLucy cried.

"There are more muffins and I've left out all the ingredients right beside the toaster for you." he said.

"But Daddy! You said you would make me an English muffin. You lied to me."

"I'm sorry Little Lazy Lucy, but I said I would make an

English muffin. And since you were too lazy to help and too comfortable to get up, I had it myself, and it was amazingly good."

"But Dad! I wanted you to make it. I'm too tired."

"You should make one for yourself."

"And Shadow is sooooo comfortable," she said, as I peeked back in the door. She eyed me with her teary and beautiful eyes. "Daddy, please!"

"Yummy yummy, in my tummy," Daddy said, as he closed the door and left his children to starve.

Displacement: A Single-Parenting Love Story

John McElhenney

"I want more time with you. More time just being around you. I miss you."

There's nothing like a little time with your child to remind you how much you have lost in the divorce. My daughter came with me to NYC this summer for a short vacation. The closeness we shared during those four days was unimaginably wonderful and welcome to both of us. It was clear, we have not gotten to spend enough time together. Even as we were walking hand-in-hand down Times Square, I was experiencing an awakening, a joy, and a pain, at the same time. Divorce is like that. You think things are going along okay, and you imagine things will continue as "a family" whatever that means. When one partner calls an audible and opts-out of the marriage, well, we are all about to take a tumble.

When I Learned I Was Getting Divorced

For me, I was asked to leave during a couples' therapy session when I discovered my then-wife had gone to see an attorney about her options. And that's really how the entire divorce went. Dads are asked to go along with the divorce, regardless of our input, and we get a standard divorce package. In my case, I lost the house; I lost 70% of the time with my kids; I was given a $1,350 a month child support payment (whether I was employed or not); I was given the non-custodial parent role (which doesn't mean much until you get behind, for any reason, on your child support payments); and I had to provide health insurance for the kids (job or no job).

I tried my best to roll with the gut punch. I fell down. I moved in with my sister for six months while I looked for a new job. (I was working freelance and making enough for one house, but not for two.) But the biggest blow, one I anticipated, was a major depression that lodged in my heart and head. I had lost everything. Sure, we were not happily married, but we were married. And when kids were involved, I was committed to stay together and fight for what we needed in the relationship. But it requires two people to fight for a marriage. When one gives up, changes their tact, and goes for the decree over the relationship, there's not much you can do but comply.

Had I known what I know now, I would've fought. Not the divorce, but the non-custodial harness that was put on me. We had parented 50/50. Sure, I had been the major breadwinner, but I was also the emotional heart of the family. I was the breakfast-to-school-wake-up dad. I was the "let's make this work" husband. Something, however, in my then-wife's family-of-origin DNA had burned out and she needed to seek a different path, no matter what the consequence for the rest of us. I'm sure it was one of the hardest decisions of her life. I do not take her suffering lightly. Choosing to leave a marriage must've been terrifying. I don't think anyone knows what divorce is going to do to them until the process is underway. And we don't learn the consequences of those decisions until much later. Like I learned this week with my 15-year-old daughter.

There is no greater loss than time with your kids.

Until I felt the closeness with my daughter this week, I didn't viscerally recall what it felt like to have her near. What it felt like to wake her up every morning and offer her breakfast and coffee. To tuck her into bed. To just be around her and hear what she's thinking. She's a bit quiet. So you have to ask questions and remain patient. But she's funny, ambitious, and curious. And when I was holding her hand a few nights ago, after seeing a Broadway play together, I was so... I was working to maintain my present-moment happiness as the ache of "how much I had missed" was also creeping along with us. I had missed so much of this kind of time with her. As I agreed to the 30%-dad offer provided by the state of Texas, I knew I was going to be sad. I knew I was going to have to sublimate my sadness and transform it into something different. I could not change the divorce. I could not change my then-wife's mind. I would have to forage alone. And deal with a lot of alone time. Time without my kids. Time away from the ~~perfect~~ family I had helped build.

A Father's Time With His Kids After Divorce

There is no substitute for time together. Over the year, I have not had a second bedroom for my daughter. Much less two bedrooms for both kids. So the kids have taken up full-time residence with their mom. There's no shame in this. It's what is. I do not have the income to make my child support payment and afford a three-bedroom house.

That's the real rub of an unfair, unbalanced divorce. Dads are given a huge financial burden. If there is a lot of money, this is merely an inconvenience. When the father is a working man, the consequence often is much more dire. If the dad cannot make the scheduled payments, all kinds of hell kick in. In my case, their mom sent her complaint to the state of Texas and the Attorney General's office began to harass and condemn me. Here's what that looks like. About two or three times a year, they freeze my bank accounts. I call them. They ask how much money is in the accounts (as if they don't know). Then they take 50% of everything I have. In the course of the next few days, my banks unfreeze the rest of the money. Effectively, I am left with zero dollars. While the shakedown is taking place, I have no money. Rent and car payments bounce. Even insurance policies go into jeopardy. This is how it is.

When the Ex Goes for Blood Money

The odd thing, the thing I have a hard time accepting about my ex-wife's decision to shred my credit and dignity, is that child support is not a debt that can ever be erased. I was going to pay her 100% of the child support regardless of the AG's involvement. But, of course, I had to have a job to pay her. When my employment got wonky for a few months, she didn't think about the consequences on my life. She merely filed with the AG and expected to be paid on time. So, this happened while I was renegotiating my mortgage with Wells Fargo. And she knew this was happening. She filed anyway. I lost my refinance options with Wells Fargo and had to sell my house days before foreclosure. Could I ever imagine doing something so destructive to her? With the potential (the certainty) of hurting my kids? No. I still can't imagine it.

Did it hurt my kids when their dad lost his house and had to move in with his mother? Did it bring me down in their eyes as a success when I lost everything? Did my son have a harder time bragging about me and my entrepreneurial spirit? Did my ex-wife care? Does she care now?

Two things I'll close with:

1. If you want 50/50 parenting after divorce, go for it. There is no greater loss than time with your kids.
2. Never file against your co-parent with the Attorney General's office. The consequences will affect both of you and, more importantly, your kids.

What's left for me to do? I talked to my daughter this weekend about setting up my second bedroom for her. "I want more time with you. More time just being around you. I miss you."

I could tell she was feeling the same things. It was a touching moment between us as we looked at each other in the Apple Store on 5th Avenue in New York City. We could discuss it more as the school year got closer. For now, we're going to have some fun together in New York. And so we did.

Section 7: The Core Promise of the Single Parent

What has happened between you and your ex-partner is water under the bridge. To establish healthy relationships with your kids, you need to let go of all ties and expectations of your former partner. What you need to work out can be done outside of any "closure" with your ex. If you can focus, instead, on the joy and happiness of your kids, you can release your co-parent back to their own higher power. It is not for you to work out your issues with your former partner. The positive single parent can pivot to solely focusing on their children and the welfare of their growing needs and future happiness.

Continuing Forgiveness As a Single Parent

John McElhenney

If I can approach the day with hope, openness, and optimism, I'm sure my joy will continue to bring joy to others.

Yesterday I got an email from the person who purchased all of my worldly possessions at a storage unit auction.

> we r so sorry, but we did not have the ability to take everything, so a lot of the personal items went to the dumpster - and most of the books r sold already, as that is one of the things we can sell back to online book stores relatively quick and easy - however if there is anything that u can thing of that u would really like back we would b glad to look for it - my wife is putting together a box with a few items that u might like - she mentioned an award and some pictures we still have - again sorry we don't have much left, but we had no way to store it all so we had to let most of it go

And a few days before that, the AG's office took control of my only bank account by slapping a lien on it for triple the amount owed in late child support payments. I say late, because I have never expressed any intention of skipping the payments, but I have been struggling to replace a job that ended in February.

Finally, I am currently living with my mom.

I know, that's the one that really stings for me. How can I head out into the world with a brave face? How do I stand proud and tall and tell my kids that better days are on the horizon? They are, but how do I convince them? How do I convince my ex-wife? And most importantly how do I convince myself, that from this low I will reemerge with a new lightness and agility? I can go anywhere from here because I'm down and out.

And yet... I am happy. I know it seems like such a contradiction, but hear me out.

I am not bitter about the divorce or the loss of my house and 95% of everything in it. My kids already know about the bank account (though they have no idea what "error" caused my -$42,000 balance, my son loves to tease me about it, he's 13). My daughter and I were going to the storage unit to retrieve my juicer when we discovered an old car parked inside my space. All of my stuff had been auctioned off two days prior to our visit. I have the notices from the storage unit for my late payment status. None of them said anything about the auction.

In the same way, I don't hold my ex-wife responsible for the divorce, for turning our affairs over to the AG's office, or for the havoc that has brought down on my credit and my life. Nope. It's an ongoing flow of water under the bridge. This constant flow of patience and forgiveness is required to continue with the joint task of co-parenting. And while we parent at 50/50, I was given the standard dad deal in Texas of the non-custodial parent with the SPO and a hefty child support payment. It's all okay. That is just how divorce goes in this great state.

And again, I state, clearly and for the record, I am happy.

You might think I'm overstating my happiness to cover up my anger and bitterness, but I'm not very good at anger or holding a grudge. And with my kids, I don't have any pretense of who I am beyond how I show up in their lives.

I show up in my kids' lives at the maximum level I am permitted. When I went into the divorce negotiations asking for and expecting 50/50 custody, I was not arguing about the child support, I was genuinely certain that we would parent after divorce as we had while married. That's not what happened, and I was given the script, "If you go to court, here is what you're going to get," as the reason we took my joint-custody plan off the negotiating table.

I'm not so sure that was the appropriate response from a paid divorce counselor, but it was certainly efficient. We moved through the divorce negotiation process with flying colors and a very small legal bill. Of course, I didn't get what I wanted, and I am struggling to get back on my feet, even with the additional house payment, that doesn't include a house for me. But I'm not so sure I got a bad deal. I've used my time off to build back areas of my life and passion that were being shut down in my marriage.

Each day I refocus my attention on my kids. Like a mantra in meditation or a prayer. As I am able to focus on my children, I can release my ex-wife from all blame in the transactions of the past. And even as many of those actions continue to have negative consequences, I am able to look at her with compassion and not resentment.

I am not angry with my ex-wife. I have faith that she is doing the best she can, at all times. I am aware of how stretched she is with a full-time job and a single parenting role. And without the court-ordered child support, right now while I'm essentially unemployed, the burden is even more difficult. I care for my kids more than I care for her, but in loving my kids more I can only hope that her life is happy and fulfilled. Any downturn for her is a downturn for the three of them as they sail on in the house that we built.

In some ways, divorce has been the biggest life challenge I've ever hit. At first, it was a wall I had to go over, as I struggled with the loss, depression, and frustration of losing so much of my world. But as I recovered my center, as I began to see the light on this side of the wall, the divorced side, I realized that my next journey was just beginning. She hadn't kicked me out of our marital bed and house, she had set me back on the path of self-discovery, alone.

I have been through almost all of Elisabeth Kubler-Ross's stages of grief since being relieved of my full-time parenting role. And the hardest part of the entire process is losing so much of my kids' lives and experience. Daily life connections that I am no longer part of. Summer beach vacations and travels that are emailed to me as pictures rather than experiences.

As I walked away from my house and into my single dad life, I took up the responsibility for my own happiness in a new way. Even with the grief and growth that was necessary to recover from the divorce, I knew that at some point I would be happy again. It was the hope that kept me strong. And today it is the hope that keeps me looking at the path ahead rather than at my shuffling feet, or back at the losses of things, and time, and old dreams.

My dream today is a happy one. I am well-fed, healthy, and heading to a late-round job interview. It has been a long summer of job interviews. And it's the hope of what's next that keeps me joyful in this state of nothingness. Other than my kids and the positive and loving relationship I am building with them, I have a simple agenda. Find the next job to support them and their mom, rebuild my credit, don't worry about "things," and move forward with my own life work.

That's the final piece of the puzzle, for me. The writing. I have always envisioned myself as a writer. I got my degree from the university with the imagination that I would write the great American novel. And maybe I have, but it's not ready for publication. I think my second novel is going to be much better.

Since leaving Dell in 2009 with the collapse of the U.S. economy, I have been writing a blog about social marketing. In that process, I developed my voice, my rhythm, my discipline of writing. I can stand proudly at this moment and say, "I am a writer." Or the even more risky, "I am a poet."

And somewhere down deep, the divorce process uncorked a different vein of writing that I had not anticipated. As I have struggled to find my center again, I used my writing and journaling to share the process with others. Often hard, often angry and defeated, but occasionally triumphant, I have chronicled the entire process of my divorce. Or more, accurately, the process of becoming an awesome single dad.

And my kids are happy. That's the greatest gift. They are not worried about me or their mom, they are focused on the challenges of a new school year. These are high times. And I have nothing but love for my ex-wife as she soldiers on without me beside her. Anything I can do to make our co-parenting experience better for her and the kids, I will do.

Last summer I was pretty sure I had solved the puzzle. I was living in a small house near a bright lake, and I would walk every day and end my hot journey with a jump into the lake. It was the same lake that I grew up on, that I lived with my parents as their marriage came apart in angry and violent sparks. But as I jumped in every day over the entire summer, I felt like I was being baptized. In some way, I was letting go of all the things that were holding me back.

I was sure that I had solved the work/life/happiness balance thing too. But I was almost to a fork in the road that I had not anticipated. And that massive change has brought me here, to this moment, on the couch at my mother's house, at 5:00 a.m.

I am happy. The life ahead for me is grand. And the new school year has just begun and I will do my best to tune in to my kids as much as they will let me. When they are not here, I will text and call and email and show up as often as I am allowed. And beyond that, I will tend to my own happiness, my own daily forgiveness, my own meditation, and walk. My journey still has many twists and turns, and if I can approach the day with hope, openness, and optimism, I'm sure my joy will continue to bring joy to others.

Prayer for All Single Parents, and Especially My Co-Parent: Humans of Divorce

John McElhenney

> "I wish you happiness in your new life, I always want to see you shine, you are the other half, the partner in this parenting journey we accepted together. Your joy is joy for our kids. Your peace is their peace, and mine. As we walk separate paths, we are blameless and grateful for the gifts we've been given. And to you, my dear ex, I give the deepest respect and love. Thank you for where we've been, where we are, and where we are going, still a family, still parents, still blessed."

I haven't always been able to bless my ex-wife. And for times in our marriage, neither of us were blessing anyone. It was hard. We tried. We worked at it. We raised kids and grew together and then apart in the process. But we never stopped trying. And I can see that we are still trying today.

I know that my ex-partner is doing the best she can under the circumstances. She always has. And though we have both had periods of struggle and doubt, we seem to be on the upswing of our co-parenting transition. I do believe that there is nothing she wouldn't do to make our kids' lives better. And I have to believe that she is always looking out for their best interest, even when I can't see it.

Somedays, I pine for being a core family again. Somedays, I look back and wonder what I could've, we could've done to preserve the respect and love that we once had. And other days I can get so mad, wishing things were different, right now. Wishing I had the next relationship underway as she does. But that's not what this is about.

This is about our kids. Two wonderful kids. The supreme focus of my life. And there is nothing I wouldn't do for them. To keep them safe, to protect them from unnecessary drama and hurt, to help them grow into strong independent adults. And I have to know that she has the same intention in mind, even when I think things aren't going as they should. It's okay. We still have our differences. And my "way" is not the right way, it's just my way. She has her own connection with the kids. She has her own path. And now we no longer share that path.

Communication is the key. The less we communicate… The more we communicate… It can be hard. And it is often the cause for friction in this co-parenting dance. So we need to take it more carefully. Answer with some thought to how the other person may react. Breathe when we are upset and want to react. It is never a good idea to fire back with anger. Never.

My anger is my own. My ex-wife does not deserve any of it. (Man, that is even hard to say.) But it's true. We tried, we negotiated a truce and separation, and now we are separate countries with shared resources. We still operate with some of the same interdependent budgets, but we've got a new autonomy. And what makes me angry is mainly my own unmet expectations. This is not the way I wanted it to work out. But guess what? It's not the way she wanted it either. So we're even. And we're in this together.

Anger is a funny beast. At first, I was afraid to express my anger. I was almost a pacifist. But pacifists get run over. And over time I learned to speak up for my own needs. And indeed, I got mad as we entered the late stages of our marriage, and when things were not going well, I spoke up. Again, today, I can feel my anger, but I can use it to change things about MY life and not hers. Anger is not an influencer for her, it's only an irritant.

It's ironic that when she's frustrated with me, I can tell. And I sort of take offense. And I'd like to respond in kind. But I've learned that I get NO RESULTS and NO SATISFACTION from being an asshole. In fact, being angry back at her usually causes me to feel sad. That is not to say I should swallow my anger. This is how I gained 15 pounds during the height of our dysfunction. But I should own my anger. It is mine.

Anger today is a motivating force for me. I can be angry at my ex-wife, I can be angry at the economy, angry at the slow-moving car in front of me, there are plenty of things to get angry about. And keeping it inside is not a healthy answer, so what is the way through the anger? For me, anger is energy. When I am angry, I can tap that charge and redirect it towards something constructive or creative. It's one of the reasons writing has become such a release. It's important not to bury it or squelch it. Anger is power; use it, but use it towards something you want.

As a single parent, there are many new challenges, things that were easier to coordinate as a couple. Now, when the kids are "with me" I have 100% of the transportation duties, 100% of the entertainment, and 100% of the feeding and handling. It's a lot. And when I'm in a bind, I can often ask for help from my ex. You can see how my friendliness and flexibility make things easier for her. Well, when I'm in need, that "friendship" is what keeps things balanced between us. When we were in the earlier months of divorce, it was much less easy to ask for anything. Today, we are still learning and still making adjustments, but for the most part, we negotiate support for one another.

Support for our kids is support for our ex. There is no way around it. Anger towards our ex is anger that ends up in our kid's world. I can take that shit elsewhere, as I do when they are with me. It's no different. My anger is my own, and it is my responsibility to leave it elsewhere and deal with it outside of my relationship with my kids, and even my ex. Yep, it sucks, but there it is.

Anger is energy. Learn to deal with it and channel it towards something you want. Any anger directed back at your ex is anger that will return to you ten-fold when you are in dire need of support. So offer a prayer. Our kids are a gift. My ex is blameless in her journey forward, and it is in my best interest to support her and the kids with everything I've got. And that's what I do.

Going for Gratitude With Your Co-Parent, No Matter What

John McElhenney

Today, I have everything I need. I may not be close to having everything I want, but my basics (food, shelter, safety, community) are pretty well covered. Today I can forgive my ex and focus on my kids and their well-being.

Every morning I wake up and contemplate my gratitudes. Often it is in contradiction to how I feel, and I use the first moments of the day to reorient my attitude. It would be much easier to wallow in the negative, the losses, the current crappy situation I have landed in. But I know the negative can rule my life. I can live in the down and depressed. Anger, on the other hand, is an emotion that I have a hard time accessing. So if I can even be grateful for the anger in my life, perhaps I can harness some of the energy that's caught up in that emotion.

This morning's meditation came back with plenty of the negative aspects of my current situation, as it does many mornings.

- I'm homeless.
- I'm alone (as it should be, I'm refinding my solo-self).
- I'm working a shit job (it's the most fun I've had at work, but it won't cover my car payment).
- My ex-wife gets half of everything I earn, after taxes,

so my effective hourly rate is somewhere in the $5 – $6 range.

- I feel the frustration of the penilessness every day.
- I no longer see my kids every other weekend; I don't have rooms for them, so I see them as I can make "dates" with them, and with teenagers, that's a challenging goal.

Somehow I feel entitled to more. I should have a job that utilizes my 15-year career and a college degree. I should have rooms for my kids, though things are a lot easier on all of us now that we're not switching every other weekend. I would love a relationship, an opportunity to be building again towards the future. And I'd really be happy to reach some arrangement with my ex-wife that takes the impossible financial burden off my daily life and ties the payoff to the sale of a piece of property that I inherited. But that's not how things work. We go through hard times, we survive, and we come out the other side changed. And I think we either come out smarter, leaner, and more optimistic, or we break and become bitter. Through the active reframing of my life, with positive affirmations and prayers, I am changing my attitude about my situation.

- I am grateful that my kids are healthy and doing well in school and life.
- I am grateful that my ex-wife has maintained gainful employment since the divorce.
- I am grateful that my mom (humbling disclosure) still has an extra room that I inhabit.
- I am grateful that I am able to maintain joy in my current job.

- I am grateful that I have the financial help of my mom, as strained and emasculating as that is.
- I'm grateful that I am super healthy and getting plenty of sleep.
- I'm grateful that my creative energy is strong and my inspiration is growing.

Today, I have everything I need. I may not be close to having everything I want. But my basics (food, shelter, safety, community) are pretty well covered. If I can keep my attitude at the proper trajectory, I can see that my current state is temporary and my prospects are ever-growing and improving. I have to believe that. I have to believe that I can find a high-tech marketing job as an "older worker." I have to believe that I will grow out of this phase of my life back into the self-sufficient adult that I thought I was, that I have been, that I will be again. It's like a prayer, really, these affirmations. I keep repeating my thankfulness. I keep appreciating what I have. I keep letting go of my expectations and immediate gratifications. And I am learning, every day, to be closer to living in the moment. I am appreciating my current life, my current job, my current loneliness. And sitting in this place, I am also learning to become more conscious, more compassionate, and more humble about what I have versus what I want.

Just for today, I will rise above it.

Cultivating Low Reactivity as a Co-Parent

John McElhenney

My ex-wife does stuff that pisses me off all the time. The trick for me has been to ignore the affront and keep moving along with my own agenda. I think sometimes she does things to upset me. Maybe she's still mad. Maybe she's spiteful and vindictive. Maybe she's unhappy with her current situation.

I'm not sure what causes her flare-ups, but they are getting further apart and that's a good thing. My winning approach has been to stay low-key.

Today and every day until my daughter is 18, my ex-wife will be suing me for child support. Now, there's no need for her to involve the AG's office in this way, but she does. With a phone call she could turn them off, but she doesn't. Something about having the lien against me gives her pleasure, confidence, assurance, something. By law, I have to pay her 100% of what we agreed to in our divorce decree. Not even bankruptcy or death gets you out of your obligation to your kids. And I've never tried to get out of it. Still, she keeps making the decision to let it ride on my ass.

Even this situation is done. There is nothing I can do about it. I've asked. I've offered alternative collateral. I've reasoned with her. But there's no change. It gives her some pleasure. But I will not give her the pleasure of watching me thrash against it. So I let it ride.

I remember when I did a personality test for a job a number of years ago. The hiring manager was looking over my results and mentioned that my "sense of urgency" was very low. "Everyone on my team has a high sense of urgency. I don't think you'd fit in very well." She was right. I've cultivated a low sense of urgency. Why? Because I like to avoid conflict, and I usually get my work done without the whip being applied. So, she did me a favor by not putting me on a team, her team, where all the projects were in crisis mode. No thanks.

So, that's the way I deal with my ex as well. No crisis. No drama. Sure, she tries to make craziness out of minor issues. She tries to escalate mundane issues. But I don't jump. I don't take the bait. I remain in my low sense of urgency and ask her what she needs from me. "How can I help?" is actually a very effective response. Often there is nothing I can do. That's the point of being out of urgency. Still, she likes to include me in the excitement. It is my choice how I want to respond.

And that's really the point of divorce relationships. You can't control the other parent. But you can choose your response. If you can diffuse the urgency and your need to be right, smart, witty, or even a jerk, you will go a long way towards lessening the drama and making things easier for both you and your kids. In many ways, a low sense of urgency lessens the stress and drama in my ex-wife's life, too. But I don't think too much about her well-being. That's no longer my role.

7 Wins for the Hyper-Focused Single Parent

John McElhenney

Some things about parenting after divorce are easier and more focused. When my kids are with me, on my nights and weekends, I let every other priority drop from my life. My connection and caring of them are my priority. And perhaps this is why I didn't really pursue a relationship the four-plus years since my divorce. I'd like one, but I'm not willing to trade-off any of the focus on my time with my son and daughter.

Single parenting has some benefits from the relationship standpoint.

1. The time you do get is more intentional (even though you don't get as much time).
2. When you are the ON parent, every item of their lives, every request they have comes to you.
3. You are always excited to see them, and as long as things are copacetic, they are excited to see you as well (there is no complacency or cynicism in our lives).
4. By having the responsibility for 100% of the parenting, there are very few distractions or opportunities for goofing off.
5. You don't have to negotiate any of the parenting decisions.

6. Under your influence, you can see how they thrive under a more positive approach to life.
7. In the OFF times, you think of things you want to share with them (absence makes the heart grow more focused).

So while my kids are with me, like this weekend, I thrive on doing the errands and chores of their daily lives. When I was married, it was often a negotiation. "You take them to Michael's for their school project stuff, while I make dinner." When you don't have that other parent around, things are much more simple. Kids need something, you provide it.

This direct approach to parenting, as a single parent, gives you additional motivation to do it right. Even as I am driving my daughter one place for a movie and one hour later taking my son for lunch and browsing possible birthday presents for him (build-your-own-computer), I am aware of how lucky I am to have them with me.

I don't resent or complain (internally) about a single thing. Sure, I razz my daughter about the songs she selects on the radio as we're driving around (Um... Iggy, no!), but she knows our connection is solid. She also knows that if she needs something (not just wants it, like a new Lululemon top), I will get it.

As a single parent, you have to deal with misses as well. Most weekends we have to drop by their mom's house at least once for something they left behind. Sometimes as a threesome, we have a hard time deciding where to go for dinner, or what to cook, or who gets to sit in the front seat of the car. But the general mode of life with dad is positive and happy. I am *so* happy to have them on the days and nights I am afforded, that there is little room for complaints or nagging.

Of course, there are some downsides as well. This afternoon,

I've heard the same CD three times over today as I've been shuffling my kids back and forth. And I've still got one last trip to go. But my approach and attitude are rooted in an unwavering enthusiasm. I am a happy single dad. At some point, I might be a happy dad-in-a-relationship as well, but for now, my kids are enough. And my time with them is undivided by any other requirement or request.

Section 8: The Recovery Path Back to Happiness

My trajectory looked something like this.

    YEAR 1: depression, financial, and survival parenting
YEAR 2: fitness, financial, and staying engaged with my kids
YEAR 3: happiness, parenting, and dating
YEAR 4: relationships with new women and still putting my kids first

Your path can be shortened considerably by conscious awareness and a committed approach to your own recovery.

How Long Will it Hurt? Divorce Recovery, the Road Back to Happiness

John McElhenney

Over four years after my divorce was finalized, I was still struck by a pang of sadness as I was dropping my kids' bags off at my ex-wife's house, the old house, our old house. I wondered, "How long will it take before I feel nothing?" But I immediately knew the answer. I will always feel a loss when dropping my kids' bags off at my old house. The rest, what I do with those feelings, is up to me.

I can sink, as I did in the early years, or I can rise and draw power from the emotional impact and love the sadness indicates. Even sadness is energy. If we let it sink us, we can spend days or weeks in a fog of sadness and self-pity. And I have to admit, I spent some time there after my divorce. And it's never quite so difficult as the time you are dropping the kids back at school when you know you won't see them again for nearly a week. What? That was not in any of my marriage advice books, I didn't know this was a potential outcome.

Getting over the loss of my kids is by far the biggest challenge I have faced in divorce. I thrive on their presence. I cajole, support, nurture, and laugh with them a lot. When they are gone, I don't have near as much opportunity for that connective joy. And of course, with teenagers, the off-time communication is less critical to them. It's still massively important to me, but they are more preoccupied with school, sports, and going steady.

For me, the time I have spent *not* getting back into a

relationship has been invaluable. I believe my inner resolve has been strengthened. I know my innate joy and passion has returned, and it's not dependant on anyone else. In fact, that's the rub. You can't count on anyone else to do the work after your divorce. Sympathy from friends and counselors is fine and helpful, but the "work" is completely up to you.

If you jump right back into the dating pool and hook up with a new lover, you might be short-changing your grieving and healing process. You might be trading in the old failed relationship for a "next" relationship that is built on the same unstable foundation. I think that's a mistake.

I tried dating again. I jumped on match.com, eHarmony, and OKCupid almost immediately after I was asked to leave the house. It was a miserable experience. There were a few cute women, but nobody that caught my attention expressed any interest in me. Bummer. But I know now that I was in no condition to date. For me it was about sex, touch, cuddling, nurturing. And those things, in the real world, come with a lot more entanglement than we might imagine.

I know now, having had two serious relationships since the divorce, that there is no such thing as casual sex FOR ME. "Friends with benefits" sounds like an interesting concept, but in practice, I always get attached. From that "cheating site," the advice for a hookup-type relationship is to make it 100% about the sex. Don't date. Don't go out. Just do it and move on with the rest of your life. Um, that's not what I'm after.

So here at four years and counting, I've had two relationships that lasted three months and four months, respectively. And while neither ended up being the "next" relationship for me, they both taught me valuable lessons.

First Relationship

I had read *The Five Love Languages* (by Gary Chapman) during my divorce, but it was a bit too late to figure out how to bridge the gap between us with some philosophy. But the information was vital to my recovery from the divorce. What I learned in my first serious dating experience was how it felt to be in a relationship with someone who spoke the same love language: touch. She changed my life. I won't ever settle for anything less than "touch." It is possible to be in a relationship with someone who has a different primary love language, but it's always a compromise. My first post-divorce relationship showed me what was possible and blew the mystery off what had gone wrong in my marriage.

Second Relationship

This woman taught me that no matter how much you want it, when the other person is not ready or is unwilling to build up a committed relationship, it's not going to work. There was no amount of flexibility or compromise I could provide to keep my second girlfriend from breaking up with me every other week. She would tell me she didn't want a relationship. She would tell me we weren't going to work out. And I would dive right back in at the first opportunity. Perhaps the physical attraction was just that high. Perhaps it was that she shared my love of tennis. Either way, I learned that no matter how fantastic I think the person is, and no matter how hard I'm willing to try, push, encourage, and nurture, if she is not ready, she is not going to be convinced that she is ready. It's not our job to get the other person ready. Either they are or they are not.

Moving Forward

I want a woman who shows up and knows what she wants. I've been very clear when the chemistry and mental acuity was a match for me. I am as transparent as I can be. And so far, I've had one near miss. This time it appeared we had a YES on both sides. Then, after three fascinating days, she went dark. Again, I could've pushed, I could've worked my romance. Instead, I listened and responded. I asked about what was going on. She said it was a timing thing, and her life had just turned topsy-turvy.

I had to accept her word for it and move on. As excited as we both seemed on Day 2, when the connection goes from 50-50 to 90-10, it's time to back off and reconsider. In those moments of reconsideration, we can have the greatest clarity. When we stop and ask again, "What do I want?" we have an opportunity to refine and redirect our energy towards what is most important in our lives.

For me, most of the time and energy has been redirected towards being a great dad and being present for my kids above all else. I'd like a relationship, and I'm still casually working the online dating options, but I'm not in a hurry. The first YES woman, the most recent near miss, had me just a tad nervous. I think that's healthy. What will happen when SHE shows up?

I don't know, but I'm excited to find out. Patient to make sure it's a solid relationship, but I'm ready. I'm asking the universe to "bring it on."

So, in answer to the original question, "How long will it hurt?" I think the answer is always. But the next part is the critical work for your divorce recovery. What are you going to do with that hurt? Get over it by sublimating your feelings with another relationship? Or are you prepared to dig in a bit, pause, and explore what went wrong? And then by building back yourself, while you are alone, you can re-find your own priorities and joys in life. When you've got someone who's ready to join you in those, and who speaks the same love language, well... I don't know, but then perhaps the hurt will be nothing more than a mosquito bite.

The Good Side of Divorce - Making Things Go Easier

John McElhenney

Sometimes it takes a third party to show you how good you've got it. This weekend a sitter asked my kids to write a simple page about why they like me. So here are a few of the things I am grateful for in my divorce (see, it's not all rant and rave):

1. We don't fight. (We didn't, but we still don't.)
2. We always put the kids first. (If I can be flexible and help her, it's best for the kids. If I get more kid time as a result, so much the better.)
3. She's a great mom, and I try and recognize that as much as possible. (She's not just the mother of my children, she's someone I still care about deeply. And she has a huge responsibility with the SOP in getting them to school, fed, loved, and cared for. And she rocks it.)
4. I have a lot of time to grow myself into a better dad, a better lover (eventually), and a more responsive and expressive human.
5. My kids and I can get silly for hours at a time. (Some of the policing she provided might not have been necessary. Now we don't have it. I'm the police, jester, and mediator, all in one.)
6. When I have my kids, I am ON 100%. (Dating and all

the crap that goes with finding a new relationship take a back seat to my kids. Always. We have a rule about waiting until a relationship is at the six-month marker before introducing the new person to the kids, but I haven't even gotten close. I'm not looking for "almost' or "good enough" this next time around. I'm looking for extraordinary.)

7. She takes the best care of them she can. (I was always amazed at the kid-centered activities she could come up with. She's better with the school activities. She's much better with painting and crafts with friends… She's got a ton of great gifts that she is giving to them as well.)

No buts.

We're done, but we're never DONE. Like it or not, she's in my life for the duration. Her eventual boyfriend-to-husband is merely a matter of time. Dr. Marriage-Divorce-Counselor said, "The deciding parent is often a lot more able and willing to move on. They've been moving on long before the actual divorce happens."

How that still makes me sad, I don't know. But she moved on. And **the more I support her "what's next," the better it is going to be for my kids.** (It might still hurt, but that's part of growing into this new world order and getting on with what is good for me, too.)

My kids are a shared resource and responsibility. My ex is a wonderful human being who is doing her best in the world. My anger is my own… and I leave as much of it in my writing and out of her life.

Thriving After Divorce: 6 Life Hacks Along the Recovery Process

John McElhenney

"I'm happier after the divorce."

That might sound trite, but I am sincerely convinced that my divorce transition made me a better dad, a better man, and a more conscious and centered man. It's been a long process for me, these last four or so years, but with some hints, perhaps I can spare you some of the mistakes I made and help you along your individual path towards divorce recovery.

Here are my six hacks for recovering your full and loving life after divorce.

1. Get Positive.

Holding on to resentment and anger is the biggest mistake I made after the divorce. I laughed when I would get in a particularly sly jab in a text response. I reveled in her long silences after I "gave her a piece of my mind." I set my own healing back at least a year by holding on to my high-road illusion. She wanted the divorce; I was the wronged party. Um, let's rewind that a bit, and re-examine.

Once the divorce is final and the deal has been struck, it's time to move on and recapture *your* positive approach to life. All the attention you give to your ex-partner, even in jest, is attention you are focusing on negative energy. I struggled for a few years with my own reaction to my ex's decisions after divorce. Get this: if it doesn't affect your kids, it is none of your business. And if it's about your ex and you, you need to take 100% of that venting elsewhere.

Don't get me wrong here. You will get mad, and you will feel anger. But the hack here is to fundamentally understand that **there is nothing else for you to work out with your ex**. There are no stupid requests from your co-parent that require a stupid and angry response. Zero. I'm still actively working on this one. But I know that my vitriolic texts or emails since the divorce have had no positive impact on our functional parenting relationship. When I smirked inside as I fired off an in-kind response, I was actually shooting myself in the foot.

2. Co-parenting is all about parenting, money, and scheduling.

Outside of those three topics, you should not have much to talk about. Sure, I know my wife has a boyfriend, and I hear from my daughter that he's nice and has a huge grove of lemon trees in his backyard. That's all I need to know.

In a divorce recovery class, I heard this idea about dealing with your ex. Treat the transactions like you would in a convenience store. You are there to get a pack of gum. You don't need to know about the clerk's day or aspirations for life. Get in, get your business done, and leave. That's the model for logistics and negotiations with your ex.

3. Flexibility is key.

Taking the flexible approach with your ex-partner will come in handy. I do everything I can to be flexible with my ex-wife's scheduling requests. Even if they don't make sense to me. Even if I don't like them. For example, after my wife had been in a serious dating relationship for several months, she requested that we switch up the parenting schedule to allow them to have the same weekends off. The arrangement actually meant that I gave up my 1-3-5 weekend plan and thus lost four or five double weekends a year. But it was a simple change that didn't mean too much for my schedule. My first reaction was, "Why would I want to do anything to help her and her boyfriend?" But my next reaction and eventual response to the request was, "Sure. Let's start next month."

I didn't get anything in return, but I lost very little. I could've been all concerned about my double weekends, or her boyfriend and their relationship. But what I focused on was my kids. If it would be easier on her, it would be easier on them. You know the old phrase, "When Mama's happy, everybody's happy."

4. Find what you love.

Jumping right back into the dating game is a mistake. I tried it, failed at it, and wasted at least a year haunting Meetup.com groups and "working" the online dating sites. It's a common mistake. You WANT some reward, some validation for being released and newly single. You want to sow your oats. You want to party. Everything is new and everyone is a potential date. Um... Stop.

Loving your alone time is the first step to getting to know what you love to do, with or without a partner. For me, those two main activities were playing music and playing tennis. Two things my wife didn't really join with me on. She put in a few weeks in the early days of our courtship because it was something I loved to do, but it never caught her fancy.

Since being single again, my tennis game has picked up. One woman I dated for a few months actually played tennis. WOW. That was a thrill. I'm willing to admit I'm powerless over tennis skirts on a cute woman. I'm learning to control my urges, but tennis is a love activity for me, so why not do it with someone you love?

5. Reclaim your joyous life.

"To find someone to love, you've got to be someone you love." — a lyric from Nada Surf's Concrete Bed. If you are still hurting from your divorce, or still learning to manage your alone time, or time without your kids, get some help. Give yourself time to re-center in your own life, your new alone life, before trying to add someone to the equation. You can't find another lover, a well-matched lover, if you've got a love sucking wound in your chest. Take the time to heal. Get the help you need. Seek professional help if you want to accelerate the process. And then rest. If we get too focused on finding a new relationship, we're going to miss a lot of the baby steps of discovering the new relationship with ourselves, alone.

6. Be where you like to be.

I've been working on this one a bit recently. If I were with a woman today, where would we be? Where does she shop? What kinds of activities is she into? If she's spiritual, where does she go for her community? If she does yoga, she's probably part of a class. If she's a tennis player, where do single women play tennis, or can I ask one of my tennis-playing women friends if they know anyone? Your next partner is already doing the things you want to be doing. Perhaps they are in a process of rediscovery too. And you can rejoin, rekindle a spiritual practice together.

Imagine where she might be, or where you might be together, and go there. Look around. Listen. Try something else.

Overall the process of divorce recovery has taken me at least four years. I've been in my happy place for about six months. If you can focus on the ideas above, perhaps you can find your inner Buddha quicker and move along into the next chapter of your life.

I've had two serious relationships in that time, and I'm hopeful that the coming year will bring a more successful coupling. But I'm no longer in a hurry. I no longer consider myself "dating" or "looking for a date." Those activities might've been helpful when I was determined to be in a relationship again. Today I'm not. I'm happy in my own relationship. I'm longing for a relationship with another woman, but I'm not hurting from the lack of it.

Get right with yourself before moving on to partner with another person. You'll be much more attractive to other healthy people and better equipped to see and avoid negative relationships.

Holding Your Dream Together as Your Marriage Comes Apart

John McElhenney

Nobody is going to hold your dream for you.

I could tell my then-wife that the next high-paying gig was right around the corner, and I could believe it. But after a few misses, she began to doubt my optimism. And as she doubted my optimism about gainful work, she also began to doubt my optimism about the marriage. Oh, we tried to support each other's dream. We did our best to encourage, champion, cheerlead, and provide loving support, but after a while, when the results just don't add up, we all begin to doubt.

So how can we keep faith in our own plans and dreams, even when the closest people around us are beginning to voice their dissent?

As I entered my second year at the big corporate job, I began to get more tired and hopeless about my future. I was doing everything I could think of to support myself while I was on the job and during my hour-each-way commute. We got a Prius so we'd use less gas and could spend a bit more of the money I was making. I started getting my haircut in this next town and sort of made my corporate base my second home base. I had an optometrist out there. I used the gym on site. I tried to eat better at the cafeteria.

But I was slipping. My blood pressure was up, I'd gained about 15 pounds during the first harrowing year. And every day I noticed more EMS ambulances in front of various campus buildings. Over lunch, I was chatting with a co-worker about the stress. "At least once a week, EMS is called to one of our buildings. Usually, it's a heart attack." WTF? I could feel what she was talking about in my gut. My growing gut. The stress of this high-paying, high-pressure job was killing a lot of people. "And over 50% of people with first-time heart attacks die." Now, I have no idea if she was right about that one, but it scared the crap out of me. I knew I couldn't stay in this corporate crock pot of stress. It was killing me.

I soldiered on for another nine months before the massive U.S. economic downturn forced large-scale layoffs. At first, we thought the ones invited to the "I'm sorry" room were the unlucky ones. Today, I'm pretty sure that my six-month severance might have saved my life, even as it started the collapse of my marriage.

It wasn't the layoff that started the spiraling breakdown of my marriage. In fact, I was pretty happy to have full pay and benefits for six months while I was trying to reorient to something that might be healthier for me and my family. My then-wife, however, didn't see things the same. She was terrified. She was anxious for me to replace the job ASAP so we could continue our current lifestyle. I needed a pause. Something in the next three months began to shift our dreams away from each other rather than towards each other.

An aside: I get it, when a new potential date looks at me and sees a man who's packing some extra weight. She can't possibly see what's going on with me. She doesn't have the concept of the me I am becoming. And she's not really interested in learning about my plans and dreams or hearing my romantic spiel. That's okay, she doesn't have all the information, she can't possibly see beyond my weight to the amazing person that I am. And, to be fair, I have a range of fitness that I'm looking towards as well.

So my then-wife couldn't hold the dream for me. She didn't see what I had in mind. Even when I told her what I was planning, it wasn't what she wanted to hear. It might not have matched up with her dream, and her plans. Where we had often held each other's dreams and best interests at heart, something had begun to shift between us. She no longer assumed that I would find the next big job. And I was no longer telling her that my next corporate gig was my priority.

I began to shift my dream away from the big corporate role the day I heard about the heart attacks on campus. I was under that same kind and depth of pressure at work. And going into the second year, I was put under a manager who had no interest in managing. Talk about someone who could care less about holding your dream. Before our second team meeting, when I offered him an agenda for the hour, he balked and refused my suggestion. Dang, my road ahead was going to be rocky indeed. Over the course of that next year I began to understand how important my time and my health were to me.

And then I was out. On semi-vacation. And what should have been a moment of relaxation and joining, turned instead into an ongoing disagreement about money. I was looking for work, but I was also setting up some consulting work that might turn into something more sustainable. But the scariest thing I did, in her mind, the thing that caused immediate friction, was I launched a blog on social media marketing.

I saw an opportunity to capitalize on what I had learned, and the company I had been a part of, by writing a marketing blog. At the outset, I did not see it as my next career, but as a way to set up my next job. I was putting into practice all the marketing and content development ideas I had previously done for other companies. And I suppose it wouldn't have been much of a threat to her if it had fizzled and not generated any traffic.

I began to hit stride after about three months. I had several consulting projects. My blog posts were getting better and better. And while I was putting in several job applications a week, I was more excited about the potential for building my own business again. (When we met I had been consulting successfully for several years.)

Again, I can't put myself in her place and interpret her actions, but things didn't get easier as the six-month sabbatical was winding down. She too had started trying to reset what kind of work she wanted to do, so now we were both about to be "out of work." Except I was still bringing in money. She was not. And perhaps that was the crisis point.

Just as I was seeing a light of possibility to get my consulting work built back up, she was starting to doubt if I was ever going to get the big gig again. Maybe that would've been easier on the family, but it was killing dad. I was at least exploring some alternative plans.

While I had begun to chart a path for my next dream, she was frustratedly waiting for me to turn the financial tap back on. I know this is over-simplifying a difficult and very personal moment of truth. But we were no longer on the same team. Somehow, my blogging and consulting was against her dream of remaining a 15 – 20 hour-a-week worker. We were not communicating very well.

For me the future was bright and I could imagine what I was working towards. For her, the future sounded a lot like full-time work, and though we had discussed it once the kids were in elementary school, I don't think that was the direction she was ready to go either.

In the end, I could only hold my dream for myself. The social blog led to a relationship blog which led to this Positive Post-Divorce blog. My dream is still unfolding. And while there is no money in this work today, I suspect that my next chapter is going to involve publishing and speaking about positive divorce and co-parenting.

I could never have predicted that my divorce was going to be the force that unleashed my writing in a new and powerful way. But now, 4.5 years later, I'm happy to be exactly where I am. And I hope that she too is happy, but I can't really tell either way. And I know she's not pleased about this blog, even as she acknowledges we have both benefited from the growth it seems to have facilitated in me. Of course, she's a much more private person.

She asked me not to write about her or the kids, ever. But, I'm sorry, that's the only way I can talk about what's going on for me at this amazing juncture in my life. I'll try to do my best at remaining focused on me, and my feelings and thoughts. And so far, one year in on this blog, I'm fairly proud of the progress I've made as a father, co-parent, and writer. Only I can keep working towards my own dream. And along the way, if I can relate a small moment of hope from this experience, that's going to be my guiding light.

I'm holding a bigger dream for myself and my kids.

Single Dad Writes to his 16-year-old Daughter About the Divorce

John McElhenney

Preface: My daughter looks just like a female version of me. I would have done almost anything not to upset the trajectory I had imagined for all of us. Now, this wonderful young lady is about to finish her sophomore year in high school. I've lost huge chunks of life with her. I lament her absence often. It's as if I were forced to experience empty nest syndrome when she was six years old.

If I have one regret, it is that I did not fight her mother for a 50/50 custody deal. We did not fight, we negotiated. The law of Texas automatically sides with the mother for custody, child support, and the SPO. I lost 70% of my kids' lives, I still make a second mortgage payment to her mom every month, and life has not been easy on my side of the equation. The good news: we all made it.

I did not send this letter to my teenaged daughter. And she does not read my blog. She knows that I write about the divorce and my own personal trials and tribulations. She will read this in her own time. I AM, however, committed to continue reaching out to her and improving our communication and setting up activities to get together.

Dear daughter, it was so great to spend a few hours with you last night.

Sweetheart,

I think hanging out is what I miss the most about being divorced and away from you for 70% of your life. But, I'm not going to make this about sadness and regret. This is about my love and pride in who you have become. In our family, we've all weathered the divorce in different ways. I got sad, over and over. Your brother got mad, over and over. Your mom, well, let's leave my opinions of her out of this. (I wish her only the best with her new husband, your stepdad.)

I wanted to share a bit of my sadness about the divorce and missing you even in the present days and weeks. But, let me start at the beginning. You see, you were a tough soul to make it down to the planet in a human form. Your birth was about a 20% chance with the blood issues you shared with your mother. We went to the neonatal surgeon every Monday morning, to see if you were going to survive, if we were going to have to do an emergency c-section to try and save your life, or some other more dramatic and devastating news.

As you know, you survived. And actually, you came out of the womb healthy and vigorous. The doctors anticipated a few days in the NICU (natal intensive care unit) for you, but all your systems checked out, your blood was red and healthy. You got to stay in my arms. And from that moment onward, you've never really left my arms. I am still holding you. I am holding you from a distance now, a distance I didn't ask for and never imagined as we grew our little family, by adding you, into four of us. Your big brother was delighted by you as well. He liked to entertain you, sing to you, give you toys, and, of course, make you cry. Maybe that still sums up your relationship to your brother, I don't know.

And that's the rub. I don't know because I'm not there. I have not lost most of my time with you and your brother, I have lost the simple, yet essential, daily contact and check-ins that come from living in the same house together. You were six years old when your mom asked for a divorce. I was shocked, then saddened, then compliant. You see, in the state of Texas, the mom usually gets exactly what she wants in the divorce unless the father takes her to court and sues her for 50/50 custody, or some other arrangement.

Your mom and I agreed to do a collaborative divorce. That doesn't mean I agreed with getting a divorce. In fact, I fought for about three months to keep our family together. (The real reason was I didn't want your lives to crack up in the last two months of elementary school.) So I stayed in the house and slept on the couch and pretended for you and your brother that everything was okay.

Everything was not okay. And here's the truth. Everything had not been okay for a long time. While I was 100% committed to the marriage and keeping the family together, the relationship between your mom and me had gotten strained and stressed by money issues, job issues (for both of us), and more importantly relationship/communication issues. But this isn't about your mom and me, this is about my feelings and connections with you. And the loss of those connections the minute I left the family house for the last time.

Dads Are Asked to Leave the Family Home 90% of the Time

I walked out of that house, never too return. It was the house your mom and I selected and paid for so we could have two kids.

That was our plan. The house was designed from the beginning to provide comfort and shelter for us to have children. And those months before your brother was born, with just the two of us in the house, it was magical. I'm certain your mom and I had never been in as much love as we were waiting for you and for your brother to be born. It's a gift from God, this miracle called life, and children, and you. You are a miracle of God, but also of the science that allowed you to survive such a difficult medical condition.

And for the next eight years, we, the whole family, puttered along, knowing in all our hearts that we were doing the best we could. We celebrated every morning when we woke you up, and every night we said our prayers with you before bed. It was easy to express love for each other at that time.

Things Changed – The Marriage Got Challenged

Money and work would probably be the biggest challenge your mom and I faced as we aspired to provide a safe and enriching environment for you to grow up in. We wanted a great school and a great neighborhood. And we wanted to be flexible enough in our work to spend as much time with each of you as possible. Of course, corporate America is not so focused on family values and flexibility to be with your kids. Both your mom and I struggled in our careers. We stayed in the nice house and nice school district, and for the first six years of your life, your mom was able to meet the bus after school. That was our agreement. That was our plan.

But you see, that left me holding a large percentage of the bag for making enough money to pay for the house, the insurance, the things/clothes/cars we needed to run a modern family. And the big corporate experience was hard on my body and my soul.

Sitting in a cube eight hours a day and working to sell something to someone through the internet does not afford much work/life balance. So, as we had planned, your mom was elected and gifted with the primary parenting role while you were both preschool and elementary school kids. It was a good life for all of us. I suffered a bit from the daily commute and corporate grind, but when I returned home each night, I was proud. I was loved. I was in love. At that moment I had everything.

When the Economy Broke in 2009

Then the 2009 economic crisis hit and my big corporate job came to an end. Fortunately, it was a soft landing with what they call a golden parachute. I was given eight months of full pay, with health insurance, to find my next job. But as I mentioned, the economy was in a tailspin. Jobs for your mom and I became really challenging to find and acquire. We floundered from January through November of 2010. When my salary/parachute ended, neither your mom nor I had a job. The harsh realities of mortgage payments on the house and COBRA insurance payments became a stress that began to unravel your mother and me in ways we didn't fully understand.

In November, I got an even better job and within a week was in San Francisco celebrating our financial salvation and getting introduced to my California team. But it wasn't only the money that had been stressed. My relationship and communication styles with your mom had become more like a business and less like a loving partnership. We were so focused on the bills we were behind on and the bills ahead, that we lost each other in some deep corner of an Excel spreadsheet. But at least I had the "big job" again.

Then Everything Fell Apart

The killing blow came about four months later when my "big job" was eliminated for some political and inner power issues between the California and Texas offices. It was one of the most terrifying moments of my life. In one weekend the livelihood that had revived our dream of maintaining our lifestyle and our family together had been crushed by another no-fault employment termination. They admitted their problem and paid me a severance, but it was two months, not eight months. The relationship between your mother and me crashed and burned in March as we both struggled with our own panic, our own demons, and our inescapable anxiety about how we were going to survive.

The good news is we did survive. In fact, I'd say we thrived. The marriage, however, did not survive. And this is the tricky bit that I want to slow down and explain to you for the first time.

- Things were dire, stressful, and unkind between your mom and me.
- Bills were growing and our combined income had just gone back to zero.
- In the crisis, your mom decided it would be better to seek security and love elsewhere.
- I did not want or ask for the divorce.
- I fought against the divorce.
- In the end, I was asked to comply with your mom's request for a divorce.

But Wait, We Parented 50/50, Why Won't We Still Do

That?

As I agreed to your mom's request for the divorce, I began to ask for how we were going to do things collaboratively. The biggest request I had was 50/50 custody. I was losing a huge portion of your presence in my life. I wanted it to be a fair split. The same split we used to share parenting duties, chores, and financial contributions. My priority was you kids, I didn't really care much about the house, the cars, or the wisps of money in the bank.

I also agreed to something called a collaborative divorce. That means that your mom and I agreed to negotiate without lawyers and not sue each other for what we wanted in the divorce. Collaborative divorce was really not what happened. We met with a divorce accountant to understand the money, and we went to a divorce therapist to help us create a healthy parenting plan and ground rules for how our lives as a family would be shared after the divorce.

I remember the day I went into the divorce therapist's office to negotiate with your mom, I can still smell and see the office we were sitting in when I enthusiastically presented a parenting plan and a schedule based on 50/50 custody. Neither the woman therapist or your mom looked happy. I didn't know what was about to happen, but in that moment I felt the world falling out from under me. I was not going to get 50/50 custody. No, by the looks on their faces, they had a different outline for how this was going to go down. I knew I was going down for the count. I could feel the depression seeping into my veins, even as I was still living in the house with you kids. I was already feeling what I had lost: a huge part of my children's lives.

Becoming a Fraction of a Dad

In the final settlement, I got something called the Standard Possession Order (SPO), which amounts to a split of time that works out to 30% for the dad, 70% for the mom. I was losing two-thirds of my time with you and your brother. My biggest fear was coming true. I really was going to lose most of my time with my kids. And as you know, your mom also got to keep the house and has gotten a sizable check from me every month to help for the expenses of raising you and your brother. That's pretty much how it goes for 95% of the dads in Texas. And, again, we agreed not to sue each other and give a lot of money to the lawyers, but... At this moment I wish I had fought for 50/50 time with all of my energy and heart. I did not. I complied. I gave up two-thirds of my time to be in your life.

Now That You're a Driving Teenager, Things are Different

It's fine that you and your brother no longer live in my house. I understand the hassle of moving every other weekend. But today, I don't even get my third of assumed time/connection with you. Your mom has won. She gets you 100% of the time. My time is relegated to my ability to offer enticing entertainment for use to do together. And you're a 16-year-old girl with a great social life. I get why dinner or a movie with me is not first on your priority list. I understand why a text from me, saying "I love you, I'm thinking about you" gets lost in the flurry of texts from your friends and even your mom, who is negotiating logistics and enforcing rules. I get it. Getting back to you is a challenge.

But I'm never giving up on you. It is my job to reach out. It is my job to offer, invite, and set up any connective time we can have together. And with all of this, I want you to remember a couple of things.

- I did not want or ask for the divorce.
- The divorce was the biggest fear in life, and it came true no matter what I did to prevent it.
- I fought for 50/50 custody so I could see you as much as possible.
- I lost 70% of my time with you and your brother because of the law, not because I wanted time away from you.
- I am still trying to show up in your life as best I can.
- I will never give up on you.
- I am proud of you.

How I Love You Still When We Are Apart & Busy

When I text you on Wednesday to say, "How's it going? I love you. Hope you are having a great day," I am doing all I can to reach out and connect with you in an unintrusive way. And I get it, you're busy, you've got HUGE amounts of homework, and a big circle of friends, and a mother and stepdad who are with you all the time. I am not with you most of the time. So, a little "ping," as we call it, is so important for me, just to say, "I'm here. I'm thinking about you. I love you."

And that's the message I want to end with.

- I love you.
- I'm here doing my best to reach out and support you, offer ways for us to talk or see each other.

- I will never give up reaching out.
- I am proud of you and your strength and resilience.

My request: When I text you, just ping me back with a heart emoji. It gives me a lot of joy. That simple contact. To you, it's a text among hundreds you will receive on any given day. For me, it is the one text I am longing to hear a response from.

You are awesome. We made it. And here comes the summer of your 16th year on the planet.

Every Single Day at a Time

John McElhenney

> One Day at a Time
> – Al-anon slogan

Today, I'm updating the Al-Anon slogan for my own use. Rather than "one day at a time," I'm transforming it into "every day at a time." Here's why.

I complain about the loss of my time with my kids. I complain a lot. I hope I'm not whining, but perhaps there's a bit of that too. I lost my kids at six and eight years old. Babies still. Malleable. Loveable. These two mini-mes were my life. Yes, my marriage was hitting a bit of a rough patch, but nothing we couldn't weather. At least, that's what I felt. My then-wife had other plans. Her pain was so great she was looking for a way out. In her unhappy mind, her unhappy marriage was a life or death situation. I'm not clear on all the details, but she was in self-preservation mode in her mind when she made the appointment with a divorce attorney. She wanted to get a clear picture of what she would get if she filed for divorce.

And from that moment onward she lied to me about our marriage. She slept in the same bed. She kissed me goodnight. She responded to "I love you" with a similar enthusiasm as before. (Not a lot of enthusiasm, but enough to be passable.) She even started couples therapy with me, while she was making plans to divorce me. I'm not sure how that sat in her mind. Perhaps the therapy would appease her guilt. Perhaps the therapy would keep me from freaking out and going postal.

I'm not sure, and she's not telling me now, but something in her fragile mind had snapped. The way forward, for her, was out. And part of her plan was to keep me in the dark for as long as possible. Her plan for the divorce was to get all of her ducks in a row (financially, emotionally, we'll leave spiritually out of the mix at this point) and tell me once her financial modeling and divorce roadmap had been finalized.

The Fractional Dad

What I got in our cooperative divorce was the standard divorce package offered to 80% of all dads in Texas. (family law varies by state, so check with legal counsel before making any financial or legal decisions):

- 30% of the time with the kids,
- a hefty child support payment ($1,350 in my case, with two kids),
- zero interest in the home that we had purchased with my down payment and kept on 80% of my salary, and
- a promise of goodwill from the ex as I became the non-custodial parent.

The SPO in Texas is what most dads are given. It's what Texas Family Law says is fair. It's considered by the court to be "in the best interest of the children." And it's based on old data that has not be updated in 20 years. Essentially, the idea is a mom is the care provider, while a dad is the money provider. And in Texas the family court wants one parent (the non-custodial parent) to pay the other parent (the custodial parent) regardless of their financial situation, or more importantly, their parenting skills and aptitude. The SPO gives moms the lion's share of the time. The SPO gives moms a hefty paycheck to support the kids in "the lifestyle they have grown accustomed to."

Dads Don't Have A Chance, Without Suing Their Wife

If I had wanted to go for 50/50 joint custody, I would've been forced to sue my then-wife. I didn't have it in me. We'd agreed to a collaborative divorce, and I was still reeling from the "idea of divorce" much less the technical details of the divorce, to understand what the repercussions were going to be down the line.

I did not sue for 50/50 shared parenting. I regret this decision today. I am told, however, that in 2010 when we divorced, I would've had a snowball's chance in hell of getting 50/50 custody unless I had gone after the mother of my children as an "unfit mother." All that to get shared custody? Nope. I didn't do it. I would do it today if it made sense.

Today, courts should start the divorce discussion at 50/50 and work from there. As it stands, the dads are set up to lose 70% of their time with the kids. And a lawsuit to change the SPO and standard custodial and non-custodial divorce would've cost me between $50,000 and $100,000 if my then-wife had chosen to fight it. Mind you, all of the cash for both lawyers would've been coming out of savings that we had put away while I had the big corporate job. The same job that had afforded my then-wife to meet the bus after school for over eight years.

Dads Making Due with Our Limited Parenting Time

My time has been limited by the actions of my ex-wife. My love and my availability to my kids have remained at 100%.

With the state of Texas behind her, my then-wife asked me for a collaborative divorce. She knew right up front, as she had been planning the divorce for months, that she was not going to give up her 70/30 split, and she knew that I was not going to sue her to get 50/50. And her lawyer knew if they went to court they would win. It was all set up in advance. I was given the standard divorce package in Texas and told it was a good deal for all of us.

With my limited parenting time, I have two choices. I can get bitter and resentful about my loss. Or I can make the best of every second I have with my kids. I chose to focus on my kids and let my ex-wife have the money, the house, and the lion's share of the time with my kids. Bummer for me. Bummer for the kids, who lost a good portion of my positive and happy influence. But that's the way it went down.

So I have every single day to make a positive contribution to my kids' lives. It is my responsibility to ask for dates, to give them opportunities to be together, to offer my love and support. And with teenagers, my rate of return is very low. Still, I can only ask. I don't have the power or room to complain or be mad at my kids. Heck, I don't even really have time to be mad at my ex-wife. What's lost is behind us. What's ahead holds the promise of connecting with each of my two kids in a significant and positive way.

Letting Go Of Your Ex-Spouse and Your Resentments

I have resentment. I can't deny it. When I talk about the divorce, or read one of my posts in a speaking engagement, I'm still hot. I'm not angry hot, but I'm excited for sure. Sometimes, I come across as angry. I'm frustrated with the way things went down. I'm frustrated that a good dad was given such a shitty deal by his loving wife and the ever-wise state of Texas. I'm frustrated with the SPO and how dads start the divorce discussion at a severe disadvantage.

My ex knew I would not sue her for 50/50 custody. She didn't want to lose 50% of the time with her kids; 30% sounded almost palatable. Painful, but well worth the freedom she imagined just ahead, as she headed towards becoming a single mom. Here existential pain was so great that staying with me would've hurt too much. She survived by divorcing me. She was helped in that survival, and in her survival planning before I knew about it, by a nice tax-free monthly paycheck. Yes, she would have to get at least a part-time job to afford the nice house. But her Excel spreadsheets checked out. It was a good deal for her. A bargain she made with herself, her attorney, and her God.

The Closing Arguments of My Marriage

Was it what was "in the best interest of the child?" Debatable. Was it in the best interest of my soon-to-be-ex-wife at that moment in time? Absolutely. I can't fault her for going with survival. But I won't forgive her for stealing 20% of my time with my kids, forever. She knew we parented 50/50. She knew we'd contributed emotionally and spiritually to our children at 50/50. She had to tell herself she was the better parent and thus deserved the 70% WIN, but that would've been a lie. A lie she has to keep to herself for the rest of her life.

For me, as a single dad, the slogan "Every Day at a Time" means I am striving to be the best dad I can, every single day. I can't wait for my teenagers to reach out to me. I have to go to them. Meet them at their passions. Show up for them at every opportunity. I am working to be a better dad, every single day at a time.

I am more hopeful than ever today. Even as I am sad about the time I have lost with my kids due to the divorce, I am happy about where we've all come and where we are all going. Remember, it gets better. And to you, dear reader, thank you for joining me on this brief tour of my journey through divorce. I hope you find happiness in all the facets of your own journey.

The Single Parent Manifesto: Love All Parents

John McElhenney

When you become a parent everything in your life changes. The world is miraculously transformed into something mystical, spiritual, and magical. For me, I was able to rise above myself as an individual and recognize the gift that happened in our lives. That process started long before the birth of my first child, but from the very moment that I helped wiggle his shoulders free from his mom's body, I was forever aware of my responsibility.

And now we're divorced. Hmm. A lot of water has passed under the bridge, but that same moment of realization and awe of responsibility is present with me all the time. As often as possible, when I remember to pay attention to this universal responsibility, I am an awesome co-parent. Other times, I get tired or distracted and I think my ex-wife is more of "the ex" than the "mother of my children." The perspective is important. I am constantly trying to do better.

I am always in the process of becoming the best ex-husband I can be. Yes, your kids are the priority, but it's important to remember the sacred bond between you and your ex-spouse. There's no escaping it. You both agreed to the deal, you both ushered in new life. And you both have responsibilities to them, but also to each other. YUK. It can be hard sometimes to remember this inclusiveness.

There have been plenty of things in the course of my single parenthood that I would rather strangle her over. However, the trick is to embrace the idea that she is doing the best she can. Always. It doesn't seem that way when things go differently than you had imagined. It can appear that your co-parent is out to make your life miserable. But in my case, that's not the truth. It is how I feel sometimes, but my feelings don't accurately reflect reality. They are just my feelings. I cannot accurately project or predict her thoughts and actions. And obviously, that is not my job. My job is to listen and respond, with compassion. Again, easier said than done, but it's a process of growth and release. As you release your ex from their faults in your eyes, you can begin to merely support them, no matter what. It's not their fault they are so stressed out. There is nothing you can do to make them less tired. But you can provide a flexible and supportive response as often as possible.

Here's the trick for me. When I celebrate the strength and resilience of my co-parent, I can begin to let go of my past resentments. One of the hardest transitions for me was dropping the blame and self-delusion that getting divorced was her idea and her fault. It sure seemed that way when everything was going down when I was asking for a reconciliation. However, today, from the 30,000-foot view back into the wreckage that our relationship had become, I can acknowledge that she was indeed doing the best she knew how. She made choices towards what she felt was her ultimate survival plan. Good or bad, the divorce freed us both up to develop into the next iteration of ourselves.

At first, for me, the loss of my primary residence and unlimited access to my kids was nearly unbearable. The depression and feelings of loss caused me a lot of downtime. I struggled. And for a long time, I tried to figure out what I could've done to save the relationship. I tried to unravel when I had done wrong, or where the two of us had broken some sacred bond. But there were no easy answers.

We both entered the marriage in order to have kids. Perhaps we compromised or overlooked some of the early warning signs because we were so focused on becoming parents. We did the dream, we had the kids, and we began our lives as a family the best we knew how.

Then, after struggling along for a few rough years, in the best interest of all involved, we divorced. We split into two houses and resumed our parenting duties.

Today, I'm closer to believing that I am happier, that my kids are happier, and even that my ex-wife is happier now, after the divorce. And even if that is not true, I can only work on my part, my perspective on the situation. I can only do my side of the co-parenting equation. Sure, there are opportunities for escalation. For the last two days, she's been trying to get me to engage in some drama about the family dog, but I simply won't bite. Nope.

I can always take the high road. I can refuse to fire back when she's hitting below the belt or complaining that things aren't working out. But I have made a firm decision not to respond in kind. Compassion first. Then firm resolve to deal with only the part of the relationship that I can control, me and my responses.

I am certain of a few things now, from this 30,000-foot view.

- I am happier than I was in the final throes of our failing marriage.
- There were incompatibilities between us that we overlooked in order to become parents.
- As a young family, we did the best we could at shepherding our babies into young adults.
- When the mystery and magic of being parents gave

way to the more mundane tasks of parenting, chores, and money, we became more functional and less romantic.

I wish my co-parent all the joy and love in the world. I can no longer provide any of those things. But I can be a soft cushion when she needs to hit or collapse into something. I resolve not to hit back. But, I won't stand-in for the drama anymore. I will only take my responsibility. I will only pay attention to the business between us as we continue together in co-parenting.

Resources

Please remember, your health is the number one objective after divorce. You are no good to your children if you are disabled by fear, anger, or depression. These resources can help you along your divorce recovery path.

The Whole Parent (blog – my personal divorce journey continues) @ https://wholeparent.org

Al-Anon Meetings (check your local listings, try Alcoholics Anonymous for Al-Anon resources)

Meetup Groups (I host a free group for dads in my local community, find a new tribe of friends)

And you are welcome to reach out to me via the website: https://wholeparentbook.com/about/

www.ingramcontent.com/pod-product-compliance
Lightning Source LLC
Chambersburg PA
CBHW071205070526
44584CB00019B/2923